Preface

Don't compare yourself to others: Everyone has their own value.

To grow and improve on your own terms. Focus on your own progress and journey rather than comparing yourself to others. Remember that everyone has their own unique path and strengths. Comparisons can be demotivating and distract you from your own achievements and potential. Celebrate your own successes and embrace your individuality

To focus on your own strengths, goals, and aspirations. Comparison often leads to feelings of inadequacy and self-doubt, which can hinder your personal growth. Instead, channel your energy into self-reflection, learning, and personal development. Stay true to yourself and your values, and cultivate a mindset of self-compassion and gratitude for the progress you're making. Remember, your journey is unique, and it's important to honor that uniqueness as you navigate through life's challenges and triumphs. Embrace your individuality and strive to be the best version of yourself, rather than a copy of someone else.

It's important to remember to focus on our own path and not get lost in comparisons with others. Celebrating our own successes and embracing our individuality can lead to a more fulfilling journey of personal growth and development. It's all about staying true to ourselves and recognizing our own strengths and potentials.

To cultivate a mindset of self-compassion and self-awareness can be a powerful tool in building resilience and confidence. By acknowledging your own worth and unique qualities, you can better appreciate the progress you make on your personal journey. Remember that growth is a continuous process, and each step forward, no matter how small, is worth celebrating. Surround yourself with positivity and support, and don't let external pressures or comparisons overshadow your own sense of fulfillment and purpose. Stay focused on your goals, stay true to yourself, and trust in your ability to achieve your dreams in your own time and way.

By Jack PK

Contents

Introductions

Don't compare yourself to others:

The book will delve into various narratives showcasing the importance of cultivating a strong and continuous self-development journey. It emphasizes setting personal boundaries, practicing self-care through activities like exercise and meditation, and avoiding comparison with others. Through stories illustrating encounters with diverse perspectives and life challenges, the book aims to provide a fresh outlook on navigating societal interactions. It highlights themes of resilience, growth, and empathy in the face of adversity, culminating in a narrative that inspires readers to embrace life with a renewed perspective on personal growth and living authentically. The book weaves together tales of overcoming slander, jealousy, and societal pressures, offering insights on resilience and emotional intelligence. Through these stories, readers are encouraged to embrace life's uncertainties and complexities, fostering a deeper understanding of themselves and others. By exploring different perspectives and sharing relatable life experiences, the narrative fosters a sense of empathy and personal growth. Ultimately, it serves as a guiding light for readers seeking to navigate life's challenges with grace and authenticity, reminding them of the power of self-awareness and continuous self-improvement on the journey towards personal fulfillment.

For more interesting contents. Here are some practical steps you can take to focus on yourself:

1. Set personal boundaries: Learn to say no to things that don't align with your priorities or values.

2. Practice self-care: Dedicate time each day to activities that help you relax and rejuvenate, such as exercise, meditation, reading, or spending time in nature.

3. Identify your goals and priorities: Determine what is important to you and set clear goals to achieve them.

4. Limit distractions: Reduce time spent on social media or other activities that do not add value to your life.

5. Invest in personal growth: Take up new hobbies, learn new skills, or work on improving yourself in areas of interest.

6. Surround yourself with positive influences: Spend time with people who support and encourage you.
7. Practice mindfulness: Stay present in the moment and cultivate self-awareness through mindfulness practices.

8. Seek professional help if needed: If you are struggling to focus on yourself due to mental health issues, consider reaching out to a therapist or counselor for support.

9. Prioritize self-reflection: Take time to reflect on your thoughts, emotions, and experiences. Journaling can be a helpful tool for self-reflection.

10. Practice gratitude: Cultivate a sense of gratitude by reflecting on the positive aspects of your life and expressing thanks for them.

11. Engage in activities that bring you joy: Make time for hobbies and activities that bring you happiness and fulfillment.

12. Develop a self-care routine: Create a routine that includes activities like exercise, proper nutrition, quality sleep, and relaxation techniques to take care of your physical and mental well-being.

13. Stay true to yourself: Embrace your uniqueness and authenticity, and don't be afraid to stand up for what you believe in.

14. Keep learning and growing: Stay curious and open-minded, and continue to seek opportunities for personal and professional growth.

By incorporating these strategies into your daily life, you can cultivate a stronger sense of self-awareness, empowerment, and focus on yourself. Remember that self-care is essential for maintaining balance and overall well-being.

1. Set personal boundaries: Learn to say no to things that don't align with your priorities or values.

Setting personal boundaries is an important aspect of self-care and maintaining healthy relationships. Saying no to things that don't align with your priorities or values is a crucial step in protecting your well-being and ensuring that you are not overextended or taken advantage of. By establishing clear boundaries, you communicate your needs and limits to others, which ultimately leads to more fulfilling and authentic connections. Remember, it's okay to say no in order to prioritize your own mental, emotional, and physical health.

To evaluate your priorities and values in different areas of your life, such as work, relationships, social activities, and personal time. Reflect on what is important to you and

what brings you fulfillment and happiness. Once you have a clear understanding of your priorities and values, it becomes easier to identify situations or requests that do not align with them.

When setting boundaries, be firm and assertive in communicating your needs and limitations. It's important to be honest and direct with others about why you are saying no and to not feel guilty for prioritizing your well-being. Remember that setting boundaries is a sign of self-respect and self-care, and it allows you to show up as your best self in all areas of your life.

Practice saying no in a respectful and compassionate way. You can offer alternatives or compromises when turning down a request, but remember that you are not obligated to do so. Trust that by setting boundaries and honoring your priorities and values, you are taking steps towards a more balanced and fulfilling life.

Set personal boundaries by:

1.1. **Identifying Your Priorities and Values: ** Understand what is important to you and what you want to prioritize in your life.

It's important to take the time to identify your priorities and values as they serve as guiding principles in making decisions and leading a fulfilling life. Here are some steps you can take to understand what is important to you and what you want to prioritize:

1.1.1. **Reflect on Your Passions: ** Think about the activities or areas in your life that bring you joy and fulfillment. What makes you feel happy and motivated? Identifying your passions can reveal what matters most to you.

1.1.2. **Consider Your Values: ** Reflect on your core values - the principles that guide your behavior and decision-making. These could include honesty, integrity, compassion, family, career success, adventure, etc.

1.1.3. **Assess Your Time and Energy: ** Take a look at where you currently spend your time and energy. Are these areas in alignment with your priorities and values? If not, consider making adjustments.

1.1.4. **Set Goals: ** Establish short-term and long-term goals that align with your priorities. This can help you focus on what's important to you and create a sense of direction.

1.1.5. **Prioritize Self-Care: ** Your well-being is a top priority. Make sure to take care of your physical, mental, and emotional health as it forms the foundation for pursuing other priorities.

1.1.6. **Seek Feedback: ** Talk to trusted friends, family, or mentors about your values and priorities. Sometimes an outside perspective can help you gain clarity.

1.1.7. **Review and Adjust: ** Regularly revisit your priorities and values as they may change over time. Be open to adjusting your goals and direction as needed.

By understanding your priorities and values, you can make more intentional choices that lead to a more meaningful and fulfilling life.

1.2. **Recognizing Your Limits: ** Be aware of your emotional, mental, and physical limits and what you're comfortable with.

To monitor your thoughts, feelings, and behaviors to identify when you may be reaching your limits. Practice self-care strategies and communicate openly with others about your boundaries to ensure that you stay within your comfort zone. Remember that it's okay to set boundaries and prioritize your well-being.

To prioritize self-care activities such as mindfulness, exercise, healthy eating, and adequate rest. Setting aside time for activities that bring you joy and relaxation can help you recharge and better cope with stress.

Remember that it's important to listen to your body and mind, and give yourself grace when needed. Finally, don't hesitate to seek help from a trusted friend, family member, or professional if you're feeling overwhelmed or struggling to manage your limits.

Here are some tips on recognizing your limits:

1.2.1. Self-reflection: Take time to reflect on past experiences where you may have pushed yourself too far or felt overwhelmed. Identify patterns or warning signs that indicate you are reaching your limits.

1.2.2. Physical cues: Pay attention to physical symptoms like fatigue, headaches, muscle tension, or changes in appetite. These can be indicators that you are pushing yourself beyond your limits.

1.2.3. Emotional cues: Notice your emotions and how they are affecting your well-being. Feeling irritable, frustrated, anxious, or overwhelmed can be signs that you are reaching your limits.

1.2.4. Setting boundaries: Learn to say no when you feel like you are taking on too much. Establish clear boundaries in your personal and professional life to protect your time and energy.

1.2.5. Prioritize self-care: Make self-care practices a priority in your daily routine. This can include activities like exercise, meditation, spending time with loved ones, or engaging in hobbies that help you recharge.

1.2.6. Seek support: Reach out to friends, family, or a therapist when you need help recognizing and respecting your limits. Talking to someone can provide valuable insight and perspective.
No problem, here are a few more points to consider:

1.2.7. Track your energy levels: Keep a journal or use an app to track your energy levels throughout the day. Note when you feel most alert and productive, as well as when you start to feel fatigued or drained. This can help you understand your natural rhythms and recognize when you may be approaching your limits.

1.2.8. Listen to feedback: Pay attention to feedback from others, whether it's from colleagues, friends, or family members. If multiple people are commenting on your stress levels, workload, or behavior, it may be a sign that you are pushing yourself too hard.

1.2.9. Monitor your productivity: Notice when your productivity starts to decline or when you struggle to focus on tasks. Pushing yourself beyond your limits can actually decrease your efficiency and effectiveness. Taking breaks and setting realistic goals can help you stay productive without burning out.

1.2.10. Practice self-compassion: Be kind to yourself and recognize that it's okay to have limits. Perfectionism and unrealistic expectations can lead to constantly pushing yourself beyond what you can handle. Practice self-compassion by treating yourself with understanding, acceptance, and forgiveness.

1.2.11. Learn from past experiences: Reflect on times when you have exceeded your limits and the consequences that followed. Use these experiences as valuable lessons to help you set boundaries, prioritize self-care, and make healthier choices in the future.

Recognizing your limits is a continuous process that requires self-awareness, self-care, and setting boundaries that support your well-being. By paying attention to your physical, emotional, and mental cues, you can better understand when it's time to slow down, reassess, and take care of yourself.

1.3. **Communicating Clearly: ** Clearly communicate your boundaries to others in a respectful and assertive manner.

When setting boundaries, it's important to clearly communicate them to others in a respectful and assertive manner. Here are some tips on how to do that:

1.3.1. Be clear and specific: Clearly state what your boundaries are in a direct and specific manner. Avoid being vague or beating around the bush.

1.3.2. Use "I" statements: Instead of accusing or blaming others, use "I" statements to express your needs and feelings. For example, say "I feel uncomfortable when..." instead of "You always make me feel uncomfortable."

1.3.3. Be assertive: Stand your ground and assert your boundaries with confidence. Use a firm tone of voice and maintain eye contact to show that you mean what you say.

1.3.4. Set consequences: Clearly communicate the consequences of crossing your boundaries. Let others know what will happen if they do not respect your limits.

1.3.5. Practice self-care: Remember to take care of yourself and prioritize your well-being. Setting boundaries is about respecting yourself and your needs.

1.3.6. Practice active listening: When communicating your boundaries, it's also important to listen to the other person's perspective. Practice active listening by paying attention to their responses and showing that you understand their point of view. This can help foster a more constructive dialogue and mutual respect.

1.3.7. Use nonverbal cues: In addition to your words, pay attention to your nonverbal cues such as body language and facial expressions. Maintain open body language and a calm demeanor to convey your message effectively.

1.3.8. Seek support if needed: If you find it challenging to assert your boundaries on your own, seek support from a trusted friend, family member, or therapist. They can provide guidance and encouragement as you navigate setting boundaries in different situations.

1.3.9. Be consistent: Consistency is key when it comes to enforcing your boundaries. Make sure to uphold your boundaries each time they are crossed, even if it may be difficult. This helps establish a pattern of respect and reinforces your limits.

1.3.10. Reflect on your boundaries regularly: As you grow and evolve, your boundaries may change. Take time to reflect on your boundaries regularly and adjust them as needed to align with your current values and needs.

Overall, setting boundaries is an important aspect of maintaining healthy relationships and self-care. By communicating your boundaries in a respectful and assertive manner, you can ensure that your needs are met and your boundaries are respected by others.

1.4. **Learning to Say No: ** It's important to say no to things that don't align with your priorities or values. Practice saying no without feeling guilty.

Learning to say no is an essential skill that helps you prioritize what truly matters to you. By setting boundaries and not overcommitting, you can focus on tasks that align with your goals and values. Remember, it's okay to decline requests or opportunities if they don't serve your best interests. Practice saying no with confidence, knowing that you are taking control of your time and energy. It's important to prioritize your own well-being and not feel guilty for making choices that benefit you in the long run.

Learning to say no also involves communicating effectively and assertively. When declining a request or invitation, be honest and respectful in your response. Express your decision clearly and offer a brief explanation, if needed. Remember that saying no allows you to honor your own needs and commitments, which ultimately leads to a healthier and more balanced lifestyle. Practice self-care and prioritize your mental and emotional well-being by valuing your time and energy. Saying no is a powerful skill that empowers you to make choices that align with your values and bring fulfillment to your life.

Learning to say no can be challenging, but it is an important skill for setting boundaries and prioritizing your own well-being. Here are some tips to help you learn to say no effectively:

1.4.1. Understand your priorities: Clarify your values and priorities so you can say no to things that don't align with them.

2. Practice self-awareness: Pay attention to your feelings and needs so you can confidently decline requests that don't serve you.

1.4.3. Be assertive: Assert your boundaries in a polite and firm manner. You don't need to give elaborate explanations for saying no.

1.4.4. Practice saying no: Start small by saying no to small requests and gradually work your way up to bigger ones.

1.4.5. Offer alternatives: If you feel comfortable, offer alternatives or compromises when saying no to soften the impact.

1.4.6. Remember it's okay to say no: Saying no is not selfish; it's a way to protect your time, energy, and mental health.

1.4.7. Seek support: Surround yourself with supportive people who respect your boundaries and encourage you to prioritize self-care.

By practicing these tips, you can become more comfortable and confident in saying no without feeling guilty.

1.5. **Taking Care of Yourself: ** Prioritize self-care and make time for activities that help you recharge and stay balanced.

Taking care of yourself is essential for maintaining overall well-being. Prioritizing self-care involves recognizing your own needs and taking actions to meet them. Here are some ways you can practice self-care:

1.5.1. **Physical Self-Care**: Ensure you get enough sleep, eat nutritious food, exercise regularly, and attend to any medical needs. Taking care of your physical health is the foundation of overall well-being.

1.5.2. **Emotional Self-Care**: Acknowledge and validate your emotions. Practice mindfulness, journaling, or talking to a trusted friend or therapist. Allow yourself to feel your feelings without judgment.

1.5.3. **Mental Self-Care**: Engage in activities that stimulate your mind, such as reading, learning something new, or solving puzzles. Challenge negative thoughts and beliefs with positive affirmations.

1.5.4. **Social Self-Care**: Cultivate relationships with supportive and uplifting people. Spend time with friends and loved ones who make you feel valued and understood.

1.5.5. **Spiritual Self-Care**: Nourish your spirit through practices like meditation, prayer, or spending time in nature. Find what brings you peace and a sense of connection to something greater than yourself.

1.5.6. **Setting Boundaries**: Learn to say no to things that drain your energy or compromise your well-being. Setting healthy boundaries is crucial for maintaining your physical, emotional, and mental health.

1.5.7. **Unplugging**: Take breaks from technology and social media to allow yourself time to rest and reset. Disconnecting can help reduce stress and improve your overall well-being.

Remember, self-care looks different for everyone, so it's important to find what works best for you. By making self-care a priority in your life, you can recharge, reduce stress, and maintain a healthy balance that supports your overall well-being.

1.6. **Seeking Support: ** Surround yourself with people who respect your boundaries and offer support when needed.

Surrounding yourself with people who respect your boundaries is essential for maintaining your mental and emotional well-being. Setting boundaries helps you define what is acceptable and what is not in your relationships and interactions with others.

When you have people in your life who understand and respect your boundaries, you are more likely to feel safe, understood, and valued. These individuals will support you in maintaining your boundaries and provide a safe space for you to express your needs and feelings.

Additionally, having a supportive network can help you navigate difficult situations, provide emotional support, and offer guidance when needed. Whether it's friends, family members, or a support group, surrounding yourself with people who respect your boundaries and offer support can make a significant difference in your overall well-being.

Remember that it's okay to communicate your boundaries and needs to those around you. Healthy relationships are built on mutual respect, understanding, and support, and it's important to prioritize your well-being by surrounding yourself with people who value and respect you.

Seeking support from others can be a crucial step in managing challenges or difficult situations. Here are some ways to seek support effectively:

1.6.1. **Identify Trusted Individuals: ** Reach out to friends, family members, colleagues, mentors, or mental health professionals who you trust and feel comfortable talking to.

1.6.2. **Communicate Clearly: ** Clearly express your feelings, needs, and concerns when seeking support. Be honest and specific about what you're going through.

1.6.3. **Express Your Challenges: ** Share openly about the challenges you are facing and how they are impacting you. This can help others understand your situation better.

1.6.4. **Be Open to Help: ** Be willing to accept help or guidance from others. Sometimes, just having someone listen can make a big difference.

1.6.5. **Explore Support Groups: ** Consider joining support groups or communities where you can connect with others who may be going through similar experiences.

1.6.6. **Seek Professional Help: ** If you're struggling with mental health issues or need specialized support, don't hesitate to reach out to mental health professionals such as therapists, counselors, or psychologists.

Remember, seeking support is a sign of strength, not weakness. Don't be afraid to lean on others when you need help.

1.7. **Understanding Your Triggers: ** Identify situations or behaviors that make you feel uncomfortable or stressed. Be mindful of these triggers and set boundaries accordingly.

Understanding your triggers means identifying the specific things, situations, or thoughts that cause emotional or behavioral reactions in you. By recognizing your triggers, you can better prepare yourself to manage and cope with them effectively. This self-awareness helps you navigate your emotions and responses more consciously, allowing you to respond in a healthier and more constructive manner. Understanding your triggers can also help you make informed decisions about how to avoid or address situations that might lead to negative outcomes.

Being mindful of triggers and setting boundaries accordingly is an important aspect of self-care and mental well-being. Here are some steps to help you achieve this:

1.7.1. **Identify Your Triggers**: The first step is to become aware of what triggers your negative emotions or reactions. Take note of situations, people, places, or circumstances that tend to provoke stress, anxiety, anger, or any other negative feelings.

1.7.2. **Acknowledge Your Emotions**: When you are triggered, acknowledge your feelings without judgment. Allow yourself to feel and acknowledge your emotions without trying to suppress or ignore them.

1.7.3. **Practice Mindfulness**: Mindfulness can help you stay present and aware of your thoughts and emotions without getting overwhelmed by them. Practice mindfulness techniques such as deep breathing, meditation, or grounding exercises to help you stay centered in the present moment.

1.7.4. **Set Boundaries**: Once you have identified your triggers, it is essential to set boundaries to protect yourself from situations or people that trigger negative emotions. This could involve communicating your needs clearly, saying no when necessary, or limiting your exposure to triggering situations.

1.7.5. **Communicate Your Boundaries**: Clearly communicate your boundaries to others so they understand your limits and can respect them. Be assertive and respectful when setting boundaries with others, and remember that it is okay to prioritize your mental well-being.

1.7.6. **Seek Support**: Don't be afraid to seek support from friends, family, or a therapist if you are struggling to manage your triggers and set boundaries. Talking to someone you trust can provide valuable insights and help you navigate challenging situations.

1.7.7. **Practice Self-Care**: Engage in self-care activities that help you relax and recharge, such as exercise, hobbies, spending time in nature, or practicing self-compassion. Taking care of yourself is crucial in managing triggers and setting boundaries effectively.

Remember that setting boundaries and being mindful of triggers is a continuous process that requires self-awareness and practice. Be patient with yourself and prioritize your well-being as you navigate challenging situations.

1.8. **Being Consistent: ** Consistency is key when setting boundaries. Hold firm to your boundaries and don't waver, even when faced with pressure or resistance.

Consistency in setting and enforcing boundaries is important for maintaining healthy relationships and promoting self-respect. When you are consistent with your boundaries, it helps others understand your limits and expectations. It may be challenging at times, especially when faced with pushback or resistance, but staying firm in your boundaries reinforces your self-worth and protects your well-being. Remember that setting boundaries is an act of self-care and is crucial for establishing healthy dynamics in your relationships.

Consistency in boundary-setting also helps build trust and respect in your relationships.

When others see that you are unwavering in upholding your boundaries, they are more likely to understand and respect your needs and limits. It communicates to others that you take yourself seriously and expect them to do the same.

In addition, being consistent with your boundaries promotes clear communication. By consistently enforcing your boundaries, you avoid sending mixed signals and confusion about what is and isn't acceptable to you. This clarity can lead to healthier and more rewarding interactions with others, as everyone involved understands the framework within which the relationship operates.

Remember that setting and maintaining boundaries is not about being rigid or inflexible. It's about understanding your own needs and values and expressing them clearly and assertively. Being consistent in upholding your boundaries sets the tone for how you expect to be treated and contributes to creating a more positive and respectful environment in your personal and professional life.

Being consistent involves developing habits and practices that help you stay on track with your goals and commitments. Here are some tips to help you be more consistent:

1.8.1. Set clear goals: Define what you want to achieve and set specific, measurable, attainable, relevant, and time-bound (SMART) goals.

1.8.2. Create a routine: Establish a consistent daily routine that includes dedicated time for the activities related to your goals.

1.8.3. Prioritize tasks: Focus on what's most important and allocate your time and energy accordingly.

1.8.4. Stay organized: Use tools like calendars, to-do lists, and reminders to keep track of your tasks and deadlines.

1.8.5. Hold yourself accountable: Monitor your progress regularly and take responsibility for your actions.

1.8.6. Be motivated: Find your sources of motivation and remind yourself why you are working towards your goals.

1.8.7. Embrace discipline: Develop self-discipline to stay committed even when you don't feel like it.

1.8.8. Start small: Break down your goals into manageable tasks and take consistent action every day.

1.8.9. Learn from setbacks: Accept that setbacks are a natural part of any journey and use them as learning opportunities to improve.

1.8.10. Celebrate progress: Acknowledge and celebrate your achievements, no matter how small, to stay motivated.

By following these tips and making a conscious effort to practice consistency in your daily life, you can make significant progress towards achieving your goals.

1.9. **Practicing Self-Awareness: ** Tune into your thoughts and feelings to understand when your boundaries are being crossed. Trust your instincts and react accordingly.

Being self-aware helps you recognize when your boundaries are being crossed in various situations. By tuning into your thoughts and feelings, you can understand what is acceptable to you and what is not. Trusting your instincts is key in maintaining healthy boundaries, as they often alert you when something doesn't feel right. Reacting accordingly means taking action to uphold your boundaries, whether it's communicating your limits to others or removing yourself from a situation that is uncomfortable or harmful. Practicing self-awareness in this way can lead to greater self-respect, improved relationships, and overall well-being.

By continuing to practice self-awareness, you can develop a deeper understanding of your own boundaries and values. This awareness can empower you to set clear boundaries with others, advocate for your needs, and prioritize your well-being. It also allows you to make conscious choices that align with your values and goals, leading to a more fulfilling and authentic life. Regularly checking in with yourself, reflecting on your experiences, and honoring your boundaries can help you navigate relationships and situations with confidence and integrity.

Practicing self-awareness involves paying attention to your thoughts, emotions, and behaviors without judgment. Here are some ways to enhance self-awareness:

1.9.1. Mindfulness meditation: Engage in regular mindfulness practices to observe your thoughts and feelings without getting caught up in them.

1.9.2. Journaling: Write down your thoughts, emotions, and experiences regularly to gain insight into your patterns and triggers.

1.9.3. Reflect on your actions: Take time to reflect on your behaviors and their impact on yourself and others.

1.9.4. Seek feedback: Ask for feedback from others to gain different perspectives on your strengths and weaknesses.

1.9.5. Practice self-reflection: Set aside time to reflect on your values, beliefs, and motivations.

1.9.6. Pay attention to your body: Notice physical sensations like tension, stress, or relaxation to understand how your body responds to different situations.

1.9.7. Stay curious: Be open to exploring new perspectives and learning more about yourself.

By consistently practicing self-awareness techniques, you can better understand yourself, your motivations, and your goals, leading to personal growth and improved relationships.

1.10. **Setting Boundaries in Different Areas of Your Life: ** Establish boundaries in various aspects of your life, such as work, relationships, social interactions, and personal time. Setting boundaries in different areas of your life is essential for maintaining a healthy balance and well-being. Here are some tips on how to establish boundaries in different aspects of your life:

1.10.1. **Work: **
   - Set clear expectations with your colleagues and supervisor regarding your workload, availability, and working hours.

- Learn to say no to additional tasks if you are already overwhelmed.
- Take regular breaks during work hours to avoid burnout.
- Avoid checking work emails or messages outside of designated work hours.

1.10.2. **Relationships: **
- Communicate openly with your loved ones about your needs and boundaries.
- Establish healthy boundaries around personal space, communication, and quality time.
- Learn to say no to things that don't align with your values or make you uncomfortable.
- Respect other people's boundaries and communicate yours in a kind and assertive manner.

1.10.3. **Social Interactions: **
- Set limits on your social commitments based on your energy levels and priorities.
- Learn to prioritize quality over quantity in your social interactions.

- It's okay to decline invitations or leave social gatherings early if you feel overwhelmed or drained.
   - Be mindful of the people you surround yourself with and how they contribute to your well-being.

1.10.4. **Personal Time: **
   - Schedule regular self-care activities that help you relax and recharge.
   - Set aside uninterrupted personal time for activities you enjoy or for self-reflection.
   - Learn to disconnect from technology and work during your personal time.
   - Prioritize your physical and mental health by engaging in activities that promote overall well-being.

Remember that setting boundaries is not about being selfish or isolating yourself; it's about recognizing your limits, prioritizing your well-being, and fostering healthy relationships with yourself and others. Practice self-awareness, self-compassion, and assertiveness in communicating and upholding your boundaries in different areas of your life.

11. **Using "I" Statements: ** When communicating your boundaries, use "I" statements to express your needs and feelings without blaming others.
Here are some examples of setting boundaries using "I" statements:

1. "I feel overwhelmed when I have too many tasks assigned to me. Can we discuss a more manageable workload?"

2. "I need some alone time to recharge after a long day. It's important for my well-being."

3. "I prefer not to discuss my personal relationships at work. I'd appreciate it if we could keep our conversations focused on work-related topics."

4. "I value punctuality, and it's important to me that meetings start on time. I feel anxious when things are consistently running late."

5. "I feel disrespected when my boundaries are not respected. I need you to honor my request for space when I ask for it."

6. "I feel uncomfortable when my personal belongings are used without my permission. It's important to me that my boundaries are respected in this way."

7. "I need some time to myself to focus on self-care activities. It's essential for my mental and emotional well-being."

8. "I feel stressed when I am constantly interrupted while working. I would appreciate it if we could schedule time to discuss things rather than interrupting me throughout the day."

9. "I value honesty and open communication. It's important to me that we can have open discussions without fear of judgment or criticism."

10. "I feel upset when my boundaries are ignored or crossed. It's important for me to feel respected and heard in our interactions."

By using "I" statements, you take ownership of your feelings and needs, which can lead to more constructive and empathetic communication when expressing your boundaries.

12. **Seeking Professional Help if Needed: ** If you're struggling to set boundaries or assert yourself, consider seeking help from a therapist or counselor who can provide guidance and support.

Seeking help from a mental health professional can be incredibly valuable in addressing these challenges. Therapists and counselors are trained to help individuals navigate issues related to setting boundaries, assertiveness, and interpersonal communication. They can provide you with strategies, insights, and tools to help you develop healthier boundaries and improve your assertiveness skills.

Therapy can offer a safe space for you to explore the root causes of your struggles with boundaries and assertiveness, as well as to work through any underlying issues that may be impacting your ability to set boundaries effectively. A therapist can also help you identify patterns of behavior that may be contributing to these challenges and support you in making positive changes.

If you're unsure about how to find a therapist, you can start by reaching out to your primary care provider for a referral or contacting your insurance provider to find a therapist who accepts your insurance. There are also online therapy platforms that offer access to licensed therapists who can work with you remotely.

"Remember, seeking help is a sign of strength, and reaching out to a professional can be a crucial step towards improving your well-being and relationships."

2. Practice self-care:

Dedicate time each day to activities that help you relax and rejuvenate, such as exercise, meditation, reading, or spending time in nature.

It's important to practice self-care regularly to maintain a healthy mind and body. Taking some time each day for activities that help me relax and rejuvenate sounds like a great idea. Exercise, meditation, reading, and spending time in nature are all wonderful ways to unwind and recharge. I'll make sure to incorporate these practices into my daily routine to take care of myself.

It's important to also remember to prioritize getting enough rest and sleep. Adequate sleep is crucial for overall health and well-being as it supports proper cognitive function, mood regulation, and physical health. Creating a bedtime routine and ensuring a comfortable sleep environment can help promote better quality sleep.

Additionally, engaging in activities that bring you joy and fulfillment can also contribute to your overall well-being. Whether it's pursuing a hobby, spending time with loved ones, or volunteering for a cause you're passionate about, finding time for activities that bring positivity into your life is key.

Taking care of your mental health is equally important. Practices like mindfulness, journaling, and seeking support from a therapist or counselor can help you manage stress, anxiety, and other mental health challenges. Remember, it's okay to prioritize your mental health and seek help when needed.

Overall, incorporating a variety of self-care practices into your daily routine can help you cultivate a healthier and more balanced life. Remember to listen to your body and mind, and make time for yourself amidst life's demands.

Here are some more ways to practice self-care:

1. Prioritize sleep and establish a consistent bedtime routine. Prioritizing sleep and establishing a consistent bedtime routine can significantly improve your overall well-being. Aim for 7-9 hours of quality sleep each night to allow your body and mind to rest and recharge. Create a soothing bedtime routine that includes activities like reading, taking a warm bath, or practicing mindfulness to help you unwind before bed. Avoid screens and stimulating activities close to bedtime, and try to go to bed and wake up at the same time each day to regulate your body's internal clock. Consistency is key for getting restful and rejuvenating sleep.

Additionally, creating a comfortable sleep environment can also support your efforts to prioritize sleep. Make sure your bedroom is conducive to sleep by keeping it dark, quiet, and at a comfortable temperature. Invest in a quality mattress and pillows that support your body and promote good sleep posture. Consider incorporating calming elements like lavender essential oil or white noise machines to enhance relaxation.

In addition to these environmental factors, practicing good sleep hygiene habits can also help improve your sleep quality. Limit caffeine and heavy meals close to bedtime, and avoid alcohol, nicotine, and electronic devices before bed. Engage in regular physical activity during the day, but try to avoid vigorous exercise right before sleep. Establishing a relaxing pre-sleep routine can signal to your body that it's time to wind down and prepare for rest.

Prioritizing sleep and following a consistent bedtime routine may take time to become a habit, but the benefits to your overall health and well-being are worth the commitment. Better sleep can improve your mood, cognitive function, immune system, and overall quality of life. So, start implementing these tips and make sleep a priority in your daily routine for a healthier, happier you.

Absolutely, prioritizing sleep is crucial for our overall well-being. By following a consistent bedtime routine and ensuring you get enough quality sleep each night, you can reap numerous benefits that will enhance your daily life. Improved mood, better cognitive function, a stronger immune system, and increased quality of life are just some of the positive outcomes of making sleep a priority. Remember, small changes in your routine can lead to significant improvements in your health and happiness. Start taking steps today to improve your sleep habits and experience the positive impact on your life.

2. Nourish your body with healthy foods and stay hydrated.

Nourishing your body with healthy foods is key to maintaining overall well-being. Incorporate a variety of fruits, vegetables, whole grains, and lean proteins into your diet to provide essential nutrients. Stay hydrated by drinking an adequate amount of water throughout the day to support your body's functions. Eating well-balanced meals and staying hydrated can help boost your energy levels, improve your mood, and support your immune system. Remember to listen to your body - it knows what it needs to thrive.

In addition to fruits, vegetables, whole grains, and lean proteins, consider including healthy fats like avocados, nuts, and olive oil in your diet. These facts are important for brain function, hormone production, and overall health. Be mindful of your portion sizes and try to limit processed foods, sugary drinks, and foods high in saturated fats and added sugars.

Don't forget about the importance of staying hydrated. Water is essential for digestion, circulation, absorption of nutrients, and regulation of body temperature. Aim to drink at least 8 glasses of water a day, more if you are active or in a hot climate.

Remember that small changes in your diet can have a big impact on your overall health and well-being. Focus on incorporating nutritious foods into your meals and snacks, and listen to your body's hunger and fullness cues. Prioritizing your health through nourishing foods and hydration is a great way to care for yourself and support your body in functioning at its best.

Incorporating a colorful variety of fruits and vegetables into your meals can provide a range of essential vitamins, minerals, and antioxidants that support your overall health. Aim to fill half your plate with veggies at each meal to boost your nutrient intake. Whole grains like brown rice, quinoa, oats, and whole wheat provide fiber and important nutrients that promote digestion and provide sustained energy.

Including lean proteins such as chicken, fish, tofu, legumes, and nuts can help build and repair tissues in your body. Healthy fats from sources like avocados, nuts, seeds, and olive oil are important for brain function and heart health. It's best to limit processed and high sugar foods as they can lead to energy crashes and other health issues.

Staying hydrated is essential for your body to function properly. Drink water throughout the day to maintain hydration, and limit beverages high in sugar and caffeine. Herbal teas and infused water can be flavorful alternatives to plain water. Carry a reusable water bottle with you to make it easier to stay hydrated on the go.

Meal prepping can help you make healthier choices by having nourishing meals and snacks readily available. Planning and preparing your meals ahead of time can save you time and ensure you have nutritious options on hand, reducing the temptation to choose less healthy convenience foods.

Listening to your body's cues is important for maintaining a healthy relationship with food. Eat when you're hungry, and stop when you're satisfied. Mindful eating, such as chewing slowly and savoring your food, can help you appreciate and enjoy your meals more fully.

By focusing on nourishing your body with healthy foods and staying hydrated, you can support your overall health and well-being. Making small, sustainable changes to your eating habits can lead to long-term benefits for your health.

3. Set boundaries to protect your time and energy.

Setting boundaries is essential for protecting

your time and energy. It involves clearly defining what is acceptable and what is not in various aspects of your life, such as relationships, work, and personal time. By setting boundaries, you establish limits that help prevent others from taking advantage of you and ensure that your needs are met.

Here are some tips for setting boundaries to protect your time and energy:

1. **Identify your limits: ** Reflect on what is important to you and what drains your energy. Think about what behaviors or situations make you feel uncomfortable or stressed.

2. **Communicate assertively: ** Clearly communicate your boundaries to others in a respectful and assertive manner. Use "I" statements to express your needs and feelings without blaming others.

3. **Say no when necessary: ** Learn to say no to requests or obligations that do not align with

your priorities or values. Saying no is a powerful way to protect your time and energy.

4. **Establish consequences: ** Make sure there are consequences for crossing your boundaries. This could mean setting limits on how much time you spend on certain activities or ending relationships with people who consistently disrespect your boundaries.

5. **Take care of yourself: ** Prioritize self-care activities that help you recharge and maintain your well-being. This could include practicing mindfulness, exercising, getting enough sleep, or engaging in hobbies you enjoy.

6. **Seek support: ** Surround yourself with people who respect your boundaries and provide emotional support. It's important to have a strong support system that encourages you to prioritize your well-being.

Remember, setting and maintaining boundaries is an ongoing process. It may feel uncomfortable at first, but over time, it can lead to healthier relationships and a greater sense of control over your time and energy.

4. Engage in hobbies or activities that bring you joy.
Engaging in hobbies or activities that bring you joy is an important part of self-care and overall well-being. Here are some tips to help you get started:

1. **Identify your interests: ** Think about the things that you enjoy doing or that bring you a sense of fulfillment. It could be anything from painting, playing a musical instrument, gardening, cooking, hiking, writing, or even bird watching. Identify what makes you feel happy and engaged.

2. **Make time for your hobbies: ** It's essential to set aside dedicated time in your schedule for your hobbies. Treat this time as important as any other commitment you have. Even if it's just

a few minutes a day, making time for your hobbies can greatly enhance your well-being.

3. **Experiment with new activities: ** Don't be afraid to try new things. You might discover a new hobby that brings you a lot of joy. Take a class, join a club, or participate in an event related to an activity you've always been curious about.

4. **Set goals: ** Setting goals related to your hobbies can help you stay motivated and engaged. Whether it's mastering a new skill, completing a project, or participating in an event, having clear goals can give you a sense of purpose and achievement.

5. **Connect with others: ** Consider joining a community or group of people who share your hobbies. This can provide you with a sense of belonging, support, and motivation. You can also share your experiences, learn new things, and build relationships with like-minded individuals.

6. **Practice mindfulness: ** When engaging in your hobbies, try to be fully present in the moment and focus on the experience. This can help you relax, reduce stress, and enhance your enjoyment of the activity.

Remember, the key is to explore different activities, find what resonates with you, and prioritize the ones that bring you joy and fulfillment. Embracing your hobbies can be a great way to recharge, reduce stress, and promote your overall well-being.

5. Connect with loved ones for support and companionship.

It's important to maintain connections with loved ones for support and companionship. Whether you're going through a tough time or simply want to share joyful moments, having a strong support system can greatly improve your mental and emotional well-being. Reach out to your family and friends, talk to them, spend time together, and let them know you appreciate their presence in your life. Nurturing these relationships can bring you comfort, strength, and a sense of belonging.

Here are some more tips on connecting with loved ones for support and companionship:

1. Schedule regular check-ins: Make an effort to regularly check in with your loved ones, whether through phone calls, video chats, or in-person meetings. This can help you stay connected and maintain strong relationships.

2. Share your feelings: Don't be afraid to open up and share your feelings with your loved ones. Expressing your emotions can help you feel understood and supported.

3. Plan activities together: Whether it's going for a walk, watching a movie, cooking a meal together, or simply hanging out, spending quality time with your loved ones can

strengthen your bond and create memorable experiences.

4. Listen actively: When connecting with your loved ones, remember to listen actively and show empathy. Allow them to share their thoughts and feelings without judgment, and offer your support and understanding.

5. Show appreciation: Let your loved ones know how much you value and appreciate them. Small gestures of kindness, such as sending a text message, writing a heartfelt note, or giving a thoughtful gift, can go a long way in showing your love and gratitude.

By prioritizing your relationships and making an effort to connect with your loved ones, you can create a strong support system that brings you comfort, companionship, and joy.

6. Seek professional help or therapy if needed. Seeking professional help or therapy is an important step towards addressing mental

health issues or other challenges you may be facing. Here are some steps you can follow to seek professional help:

1. **Recognize the need: ** Acknowledge that you may benefit from talking to a professional. This could be due to symptoms of a mental health condition, relationship issues, stress, trauma, or any other challenges you are experiencing.

2. **Research: ** Look for different types of therapy and professionals in your area. You can search online, ask for recommendations from your primary care physician, or seek referrals from friends and family.

3. **Choose the right therapist: ** Consider the type of therapy that may work best for you (such as cognitive-behavioral therapy, psychodynamic therapy, etc.) and find a therapist who specializes in treating the issues you are facing.

4. **Contact the therapist: ** Reach out to the therapist or counseling center to schedule an appointment. Many therapists offer a free initial consultation or phone call to discuss your needs and see if they are a good fit for you.

5. **Prepare for the first session: ** Before your first session, think about what you want to discuss and any goals you have for therapy. It's okay if you're not sure; your therapist will guide you through the process.

6. **Be open and honest: ** During therapy sessions, be open and honest with your therapist about your thoughts, feelings, and experiences. Therapy is a safe space for you to explore your concerns and work towards healing and personal growth.

7. **Follow the treatment plan: ** Your therapist may recommend certain exercises, activities, or techniques to help you make progress. It's important to actively participate in your

therapy and practice what you learn outside of sessions.

Remember that seeking help is a brave and important step towards taking care of your mental health. If you're in crisis or need immediate help, don't hesitate to reach out to a crisis hotline, a mental health professional, or go to the nearest emergency room for assistance. You deserve to receive the support and care you need.

7. Practice mindfulness and being present in the moment.

One way to practice mindfulness and be present in the moment is through focusing on your breath. Find a quiet place, sit or lie down comfortably, and pay attention to each breath as you inhale and exhale. Another way is to engage in mindful activities such as walking in nature, eating a meal slowly and savoring each bite, or practicing yoga or meditation. Simply notice your thoughts and feelings without judgment and bring your awareness back to the present moment whenever your mind starts to wander. Consistent practice can help you cultivate a sense of calm and focus in your daily life.

Mindful breathing and engaging in mindfulness activities, you can also try body scan meditations, where you systematically focus on each part of your body, starting from your toes all the way up to your head, noticing any sensations without trying to change them. Another helpful practice is to incorporate mindfulness into daily routines, such as mindful washing of dishes or brushing your teeth, fully immersing yourself in the present moment. Practicing gratitude and self-compassion can also help you stay present and appreciate the current moment. Remember, mindfulness is a skill that can be developed over time with practice and patience.

Practicing mindfulness involves being fully present and engaged in the current moment.

Here are some steps to help you practice mindfulness:

1. **Start with your breath**: Focus on your breath as it moves in and out of your body. This can help anchor you in the present moment.

2. **Observe your surroundings**: Use your senses to pay attention to your environment. Notice the sights, sounds, smells, and sensations around you without judgment.

3. **Stay present**: When your mind starts to wander, gently bring your attention back to the present moment. You can do this by focusing on your breath or the sensations in your body.

4. **Engage in mindful activities**: Practice mindfulness while doing everyday activities such as eating, walking, or washing dishes. Pay full attention to these activities and appreciate the experience.

5. **Practice regularly**: Set aside time each day to practice mindfulness. This could be through

meditation, yoga, or simply taking a few minutes to focus on the present moment.
Remember, mindfulness is a skill that takes practice. Be patient with yourself and keep trying, even if it feels challenging at first.

8. Take breaks when needed and avoid overcommitting yourself.
Taking breaks and avoiding overcommitting yourself are important for maintaining your well-being and productivity. Here are some tips on how to achieve that:

1. **Listen to your body and mind**: Pay attention to any signs of fatigue, burnout, or stress. If you start feeling overwhelmed or exhausted, it's a clear sign that you need to take a break.

2. **Schedule regular breaks**: Incorporate short breaks throughout your day to rest and recharge. This could be a 5–10-minute break every hour or a longer break in the middle of the day. Find what works best for you.

3. **Set boundaries**: Learn to say no when you already have a full plate. Prioritize your commitments and don't take on more than you can handle.

4. **Practice time management**: Plan your day effectively, allocate time for tasks, and avoid overcommitting yourself by being realistic about what you can accomplish in a day.

5. **Delegate tasks**: If possible, delegate some of your responsibilities to others. It's okay to ask for help when needed.

6. **Take care of yourself**: Make sure to get enough sleep, eat well, exercise regularly, and engage in activities that help you relax and unwind.

7. **Mindfulness and relaxation techniques**: Practice mindfulness, meditation, deep breathing, or other relaxation techniques to help manage stress and stay focused.

8. **Reflect and adjust**: Regularly reflect on your commitments and workload. If you find yourself consistently overcommitted, reassess your priorities and make necessary adjustments.

Remember, it's essential to prioritize self-care and set boundaries to avoid burning out. Taking breaks and managing your commitments effectively will help you maintain a healthy work-life balance.

9. Treat yourself with compassion and kindness.

Treating yourself with compassion and kindness is essential for overall well-being and happiness. Here are some tips on how to practice self-compassion:

1. **Practice self-awareness**: Be mindful of your thoughts and feelings. Notice when you are being self-critical and try to replace those

negative thoughts with more positive and self-compassionate ones.

2. **Be kind to yourself**: Treat yourself the way you would treat a friend in need. Offer yourself words of encouragement, support, and kindness.

3. **Practice self-care**: Take care of your physical and emotional needs. Make time for activities that bring you joy and relaxation. This can be anything from exercise, meditation, taking a bath, reading a book, or spending time with loved ones.

4. **Forgive yourself**: Everyone makes mistakes. Instead of being hard on yourself for your imperfections, acknowledge them and learn from them. Practice self-forgiveness and let go of any guilt or shame.

5. **Set boundaries**: Learn to say no to things that drain your energy or cause you stress. Set boundaries that prioritize your well-being and

give yourself permission to prioritize your needs.

6. **Practice gratitude**: Focus on the positive aspects of your life and cultivate gratitude for all that you have. Remind yourself of your strengths, accomplishments, and the things that make you unique.

7. **Seek support**: Talk to friends, family, or a therapist about your feelings and struggles. Sometimes, sharing your thoughts with others can provide you with a new perspective and offer emotional support.

8. **Practice self-compassion exercises**: Engage in activities like loving-kindness meditation or journaling to enhance self-compassion and develop a more positive self-image.

Remember, self-compassion is a journey, and it takes practice to cultivate this mindset. Be patient with yourself and remember that you deserve love and kindness, just like anyone else.

10. Remember that self-care is a continuous process, so make it a regular part of your routine.

Self-care can take many forms, such as getting enough sleep, eating nutritious foods, exercising regularly, practicing mindfulness or meditation, setting boundaries, seeking support from loved ones, engaging in hobbies you enjoy, and taking time for relaxation and rest. It's essential to listen to your body and mind, and prioritize activities that promote your physical, emotional, and mental health. By making self-care a regular part of your routine, you can better manage stress, boost your mood, increase your productivity, and enhance your overall quality of life. Remember that self-care is not a luxury but a necessity, so be sure to prioritize your well-being and make time for yourself every day.

Absolutely! Self-care is an ongoing journey that requires continuous effort and attention. It's about nurturing yourself and tending to your needs in a way that promotes balance and well-being in your life. Remember that self-care is not selfish; it's about taking care of yourself so that you can show up as the best version of yourself in all areas of your life.

Incorporating self-care practices into your routine can help you build resilience, manage stress more effectively, improve your relationships, and enhance your overall quality of life. Whether it's a small act of self-care like enjoying a cup of tea in the morning or a more significant investment in yourself such as seeking therapy or counseling, every effort you make towards prioritizing your well-being is valuable.

Don't forget to set boundaries in your life to protect your time and energy, and learn to say no when necessary. Surround yourself with supportive and positive influences, and don't hesitate to seek help or guidance when you need it. Remember that self-care is a journey of self-discovery and growth, so be patient and kind to yourself along the way. Your well-being is worth the investment, so make self-care a priority in your life and watch yourself thrive.

Here are some additional self-care practices you can incorporate into your routine to further enhance your well-being:

1. **Physical Activity**: Engage in regular exercise or movement that you enjoy, whether it's yoga, walking, dancing, or any other form of physical activity. Physical movement can boost your mood and energy levels.

2. **Mindfulness and Relaxation**: Practice mindfulness techniques such as deep breathing, meditation, or progressive muscle relaxation to help calm your mind and reduce stress.

3. **Healthy Eating**: Nourish your body with balanced meals and stay hydrated. Eating nutritious foods can have a positive impact on both your physical and mental health.

4. **Quality Sleep**: Prioritize getting enough restful sleep each night to refresh your body and mind. Establishing a bedtime routine and creating a comfortable sleep environment can support better sleep.

5. **Engage in Hobbies**: Make time for activities you enjoy, whether it's painting, reading, gardening, or anything that brings you joy and relaxation.

6. **Connect with Others**: Foster meaningful relationships with friends, family, or support groups. Social connections can provide emotional support and a sense of belonging.

7. **Unplug and Disconnect**: Take breaks from technology and social media to give your mind a rest and focus on the present moment.

8. **Nature and Outdoors**: Spend time in nature, whether it's going for a hike, visiting a park, or simply sitting outside. Nature can have a calming and rejuvenating effect on your well-being.

9. **Journaling**: Keep a journal to reflect on your thoughts and emotions, set goals, or simply express yourself freely.

10. **Professional Support**: If needed, don't hesitate to seek the help of a therapist, counselor, or healthcare professional to work through challenges and prioritize your mental health.

"Remember that self-care is a personal journey, and it's essential to find what works best for you. By making self-care a priority and integrating these practices into your routine, you can nurture your well-being and cultivate resilience in the face of life's challenges."

3. Identify your goals and priorities:

Determine what is important to you and set clear goals to achieve them.

"Identify your goals and priorities" means taking the time to determine what is most important to you and what you want to achieve in your life. This involves setting specific objectives and deciding on the actions that will help you work towards those objectives. By understanding your goals and priorities, you can focus your efforts and make decisions that align with what matters most to you.

Understanding your goals and priorities can provide guidance and direction in both short-term and long-term decision-making. It helps you stay motivated and focused, as you have a clear picture of what you are working towards. By identifying your goals, you can create a plan of action and break down larger objectives into smaller, manageable tasks.

Prioritizing your goals allows you to allocate your time, energy, and resources effectively. By determining what is most important to you, you can make informed choices about how to spend your time and which opportunities to pursue. This can lead to increased productivity, a sense of accomplishment, and a greater sense of fulfillment in both your personal and professional life.

In summary, identifying your goals and priorities involves self-reflection, goal-setting, and strategic planning. It empowers you to make decisions that are in alignment with your values and aspirations, leading to a more purposeful and fulfilling life.

Identifying your goals and priorities is an important step in planning and achieving success in various aspects of your life. Here are some steps you can take to help identify your goals and priorities:

3.1. Self-reflection: Take some time to reflect on your values, interests, and strengths. Think about what truly matters to you and what you want to achieve in different areas of your life, such as career, relationships, health, and personal development.

Self-reflection is a valuable practice that can help you gain insight into your thoughts, feelings, and behaviors, leading to personal growth and development. Here are some steps to engage in self-reflection:

3.1.1. **Create a routine: ** Set aside dedicated time regularly to reflect on your experiences and actions. This could be daily, weekly, or monthly, depending on your preference.

3.1.2. **Find a quiet space: ** Choose a quiet and comfortable environment where you can focus without distractions.

3.1.3. **Ask yourself questions: ** Think about questions that prompt deep thinking, such as "What are my strengths and weaknesses?", "What emotions am I feeling?", "What could I have done differently in this situation?", or "What are my goals and aspirations?"

3.1.4. **Journal: ** Write down your thoughts, feelings, and reflections in a journal. This can help you organize your thoughts and track your progress over time.

3.1.5. **Be honest with yourself: ** Practice self-honesty and try to see yourself as objectively as possible. Acknowledge both your successes and areas for improvement.

3.1.6. **Acknowledge your emotions: ** Pay attention to your emotional responses during self-reflection. Understanding your emotions can provide valuable insights into your inner workings.

3.1.7. **Set goals: ** Use your reflections to set specific, achievable goals for personal growth and development.

3.1.8. **Practice self-compassion: ** Be kind to yourself during the self-reflection process. Recognize that everyone has areas for improvement and that self-reflection is a tool for growth, not self-criticism.

By engaging in self-reflection regularly, you can gain a deeper understanding of yourself, your values, and your goals, leading to personal insight and growth.

3.2. Set SMART goals: Make your goals Specific, Measurable, Achievable, Relevant, and Time-bound. This will help you create tangible targets and track your progress effectively.

Setting SMART goals for yourself involves making goals that are Specific, Measurable, Achievable, Relevant, and Time-bound. Here's how you can set SMART goals:

3.2.1. Specific: Clearly define what you want to achieve. Be specific about your goal and avoid vague language.

3.2.2. Measurable: Make sure you can quantify or measure your goal so that you know when you have achieved it.

3.2.3. Achievable: Your goal should be realistic and attainable within your skills, resources, and timeframe.

3.2.4. Relevant: Ensure that your goal aligns with your overall objectives and is meaningful to you.

3.2.5. Time-bound: Set a deadline or time frame for achieving your goal to create a sense of urgency and focus.

By following these SMART criteria, you can set effective goals that are clear, actionable, and achievable.

3.3. Prioritize: Once you have a list of goals, prioritize them based on their importance and impact on your life. Consider which goals are more urgent or align better with your long-term vision.

Prioritizing tasks is essential for effective time management and productivity. By organizing tasks based on their importance and deadlines, you can focus on important and urgent tasks first to maximize efficiency. It's helpful to create to-do lists, set deadlines, and break down larger tasks into smaller, more manageable ones. Remember to allocate time for both important tasks and those that are time-sensitive to maintain a balanced approach to task management.

When prioritizing tasks, it's important to consider the urgency and importance of each item on your to-do list. One common method is the Eisenhower Matrix, which categorizes tasks into four quadrants based on their urgency and importance. By identifying and focusing on tasks that are both urgent and important, you can address critical needs first. Additionally, setting clear goals, using tools like time blocking or Pomodoro Technique, and regularly reviewing and adjusting priorities can help you stay organized and focused on what matters most. Remember to be flexible and adapt your priorities as needed to maintain a balance between important tasks and urgent deadlines.

Prioritizing is a skill that involves organizing tasks, activities, or goals in order of importance or urgency. Here are some steps to help you prioritize effectively:

3.3.1. **Make a List**: Write down all the tasks or goals that you need to prioritize. Having a clear list can help you visualize everything that needs to be done.

3.3.2. **Identify Urgency**: Determine which tasks are time-sensitive or have a deadline. These tasks should be given higher priority.

3.3.3. **Assess Importance**: Evaluate the importance of each task in relation to your goals, objectives, or values. Focus on tasks that align with your long-term priorities.

3.3.4. **Consider Effort**: Consider the effort required for each task. Some tasks may be quick and easy to accomplish, while others may be more complex and time-consuming.

3.3 5. **Use a Priority Matrix**: You can use a matrix like the Eisenhower Matrix (based on urgency and importance) to categorize tasks into quadrants: urgent and important, urgent but not important, important but not urgent, not urgent and not important.

3.3.6. **Focus on High-Value Tasks**: Give priority to tasks that will have a significant impact on your goals or projects.

3.3.7. **Delegate or eliminate**: If possible, delegate tasks to others or eliminate tasks that are not necessary or do not align with your goals.

3.3.8. **Review and adjust**: Regularly review your priorities and adjust them as needed based on changing circumstances or new information.

Remember, prioritizing is a skill that takes practice, so be patient with yourself as you work on improving your ability to prioritize effectively.

3.4. Consider your values: Your values act as a guiding force in setting priorities. Ensure that your goals are in alignment with your values to create a sense of purpose and fulfillment.

Your values act as a guiding force in setting priorities by helping you determine what truly matters to you. When you align your priorities with your values, you ensure that your time and energy are focused on what brings you fulfillment and satisfaction. Reflecting on your values can provide clarity on what is most important to you, allowing you to make decisions that are in line with your beliefs and principles. By prioritizing based on your values, you create a sense of purpose and direction in your life, leading to greater fulfillment and personal growth.

Values are deeply held beliefs and principles that guide a person's behavior and decision-making. They help shape our attitudes, priorities, and actions in various aspects of life. Values are important because they determine how we interact with others, how we approach challenges, and what we consider important or meaningful. By understanding and reflecting on our values, we are better equipped to make choices that align with our authentic selves and lead to a more fulfilling life.

Values are often shaped by a combination of factors, including cultural influences, personal experiences, upbringing, and societal norms. Some common values that individuals may hold include honesty, integrity, respect, compassion, fairness, empathy, loyalty, and kindness. Understanding our values can help us clarify what is truly important to us and guide us in making decisions that are in alignment with those values.

It is helpful to regularly reflect on and assess our values to ensure that they are still relevant and meaningful to us. This self-awareness can help us navigate difficult situations, make ethical choices, and live a more authentic and purposeful life. Additionally, understanding our values can also help us in building stronger relationships with others who share similar values or in finding common ground with those who hold different ones.

In a broader sense, considering our values means recognizing the core principles that we hold dear and allowing them to inform our thoughts, actions, and interactions with the world. By living in accordance with our values, we can cultivate a sense of integrity, authenticity, and fulfillment, leading to a more meaningful and purpose-driven life.

3.5. Time management: Understand how much time you can realistically allocate to different goals and prioritize them accordingly. This will help you focus on what matters most.

Effective time management involves understanding your priorities and goals, and then allocating your time accordingly. Here are some steps you can take to manage your time effectively:

3.5.1. **Set SMART goals**: Make sure your goals are Specific, Measurable, Achievable, Relevant, and Time-bound. This will help you focus your efforts on what truly matters.

3.5.2. **Prioritize tasks**: Identify tasks that are urgent and important, and focus on those first. Use techniques like the Eisenhower Matrix to categorize tasks as urgent, important, low priority, or time-wasters.

3.5.3. **Create a schedule**: Plan your day or week ahead of time. Allocate blocks of time for specific tasks or activities. Be realistic about how much time each task will take.

3.5.4. **Avoid multitasking**: While it may seem like you're getting more done, multitasking can actually decrease productivity. Focus on one task at a time to improve efficiency and quality of work.

3.5.5. **Take breaks**: Schedule regular breaks to rest and recharge. This can help you maintain focus and avoid burnout.

3.5.6. **Eliminate distractions**: Identify and eliminate sources of distraction that prevent you from staying focused on your tasks.

3.5.7. **Review and adjust**: Regularly review your progress and adjust your schedule as needed. Be flexible in adapting to changes and unexpected events.

By following these steps and adjusting your approach as needed, you can develop effective time management skills to help you reach your goals and make the most of your time.

3.6. Seek feedback: Discuss your goals and priorities with trusted friends, family members, mentors, or coaches. Getting different perspectives can help you gain clarity and refine your goals.

Seeking feedback from trusted friends, family members, mentors, or coaches can be incredibly valuable when it comes to discussing your goals and priorities. These individuals can offer fresh perspectives, insights, and advice that you may not have considered on your own. By opening up the conversation and actively listening to their feedback, you can gain clarity, refine your goals, and potentially uncover new opportunities or challenges that you hadn't initially thought about.

When seeking feedback, it's important to choose individuals who you trust and who have your best interests at heart. They should be able to provide constructive criticism, support, and guidance to help you navigate your goals effectively. By sharing your aspirations with others, you open yourself up to new ideas, different viewpoints, and potential solutions that can further enhance your understanding of your goals and how to achieve them.

Remember that feedback is an essential part of personal growth and development. Embrace the input you receive from others, reflect on it, and use it to make informed decisions moving forward. With the support and insights of your trusted circle, you can refine your goals, prioritize effectively, and create a plan that aligns with your aspirations and values.

3.7. Review and adjust: Regularly review your goals and priorities to ensure they still align with your values and long-term vision. Be open

to adjusting them as needed based on changing circumstances or new insights.

This advice encourages individuals to stay conscious of their goals and priorities by reviewing them regularly. It also emphasizes the importance of ensuring that these goals are aligned with one's values and long-term vision. Additionally, it suggests being flexible and open to adjusting goals when necessary due to changing circumstances or newfound perspectives. This approach promotes self-awareness, adaptability, and growth in pursuing one's aspirations.

By consistently revisiting your goals and priorities, you establish a framework for self-reflection and self-improvement. This practice enables you to stay focused on what truly matters to you and ensures that your actions are in line with your values and aspirations. Being open to adjusting your goals shows a willingness to adapt to new information and circumstances, fostering resilience and agility in the face of change.

Regularly assessing and refining your goals can lead to greater clarity, motivation, and fulfillment in your pursuits. It empowers you to make intentional choices that support your long-term vision and promote personal growth.

"Remember that goal-setting is not a rigid process; it's a dynamic and continuous journey of self-discovery and progress. Embrace the opportunity to fine-tune your goals as you evolve and learn more about yourself and the world around you."

4. Limit distractions:

Reduce time spent on social media or other activities that do not add value to your life.

"Limit distractions" means to reduce or minimize anything that may divert your attention from a task or activity. This could include turning off notifications on your phone, finding a quiet workspace, or setting boundaries with other people to create a focused and productive environment. By limiting distractions, you can enhance your ability to concentrate and be more efficient in completing your tasks.

Limiting distractions is crucial in today's fast-paced world where we are constantly bombarded with information from various sources. By taking proactive steps to limit distractions, you can improve your focus, increase productivity, and reduce feelings of overwhelm or stress. This could involve setting specific times for checking emails or social media, creating a clutter-free workspace, using focus-enhancing techniques like the Pomodoro Technique, or practicing mindfulness to stay present and attentive to the task at hand. The key is to identify what distracts you the most and implement strategies to minimize their impact, allowing you to work more efficiently and effectively towards your goals.

To reduce time spent on social media or other activities that do not add value to your life, you can try the following strategies:

4.1. Set specific time limits: Allocate a certain amount of time each day for these activities and stick to it. Use phone settings or apps to track and limit your usage.

Setting specific time limits can be achieved in various ways depending on what you need the time limits for. Here are a few common scenarios with suggestions on how to set specific time limits:

4.1.1. **Daily Routine**: If you want to set time limits for specific activities during your day, you can use a planner or scheduling app to allocate a certain amount of time for each task.

4.1.2. **Work Tasks**: Use time management techniques like the Pomodoro Technique, where you work for a set amount of time (e.g., 25 minutes) and then take a short break. There are apps like Toggl and Forest that can help you track and manage your time.

4.1.3. **Meetings and Discussions**: Setting time limits for meetings can help keep discussions focused and efficient. As a meeting organizer, you can set an agenda with time slots for each topic and make sure to stick to them.

4.1.4. **Screen Time**: If you want to limit your screen time on devices, you can use built-in features like Screen Time on iOS devices or apps like Freedom or StayFocus on desktops to set specific time limits for different apps or websites.

4.1.5. **Parental Controls**: To limit screen time for kids, you can use parental control features available on devices or use tools like Qustodio or Bark to set specific time limits on devices and apps.

4.1.6. **Studying or Research**: If you need to limit the time spent on research or studying, consider setting a timer or using website blockers like Cold Turkey to restrict access after a certain period.

Remember, setting specific time limits can help you stay organized, focused, and improve productivity. Experiment with different tools and techniques to find what works best for you in different situations.

4.2. Identify triggers: Recognize what prompts you to engage in these activities excessively, whether it's boredom, stress, or habit, and find alternative ways to address those triggers.

Here are some common triggers and alternative strategies to address them:

4.2.1. Boredom: If you find yourself engaging in activities excessively due to boredom, try to find new hobbies or activities that interest you. Engaging in creative pursuits, exercise, or social activities can help alleviate boredom.

4.2.2. Stress: Some people may overindulge in certain activities as a way to cope with stress. Instead of relying on these activities, consider stress-relief techniques such as deep breathing, mindfulness meditation, or physical exercise.

4.2.3. Habit: Sometimes excessive engagement in certain activities becomes a habit that is hard to break. To address this, try to replace the negative habit with a positive one. For example, if you tend to overeat out of habit, try replacing it with healthier snacking options or drinking water instead.

4.2.4. Emotional triggers: Emotions like loneliness, sadness, or anxiety can also trigger excessive engagement in certain activities. In such cases, it's important to address the underlying emotional issues through therapy, talking to someone you trust, or practicing self-care.

4.2.5. Environment: Sometimes your physical surroundings can trigger excessive engagement in certain activities. If, for example, your work environment or social circle encourages certain behaviors, consider making changes to your surroundings or creating boundaries to avoid triggers.

4.2.6. Social pressure: Peer pressure or social norms can also drive excessive engagement in activities. If you find yourself engaging in activities excessively to fit in or please others, focus on building self-confidence and setting boundaries to prioritize your well-being.

4.2.7. Lack of fulfillment: If you are engaging in activities excessively because you feel unfulfilled in other areas of your life, it's important to identify what is missing and work towards addressing those needs. This could involve setting goals, pursuing passions, or seeking professional help if needed.

4.2.8. Mindfulness and reflection: Practice mindfulness to become more aware of your thoughts, emotions, and triggers that lead to excessive behavior. Reflect on your actions and motivations to understand why you engage in certain activities excessively and explore healthier alternatives.

4.2.9. Self-care and stress management: Prioritize self-care practices such as getting enough sleep, eating well, exercising, and managing stress effectively. Building a strong foundation of self-care can help reduce the likelihood of turning to excessive activities as a coping mechanism.

By identifying your triggers and finding healthier alternatives to address them, you can work towards breaking patterns of excessiveness and promoting a more balanced lifestyle. If you need further assistance or guidance, feel free to ask.

4.3. Prioritize meaningful activities: Focus on activities that align with your goals, values, and overall well-being. Engage in hobbies, exercise, learning, or spending time with loved ones instead.

Prioritizing meaningful activities involves identifying your values and goals, then allocating your time and energy accordingly. To do this effectively, start by creating a list of all your activities and tasks, then rank them based on their alignment with your values and long-term goals. Consider the impact each activity has on your well-being, relationships, personal growth, and overall happiness. Focus on activities that bring you fulfillment, purpose, and joy, and be willing to let go of tasks that do not contribute significantly to your well-being. Regularly review and adjust your priorities to ensure you are dedicating time to what truly matters to you.

Taking time to engage in activities that align with your goals, values, and overall well-being is essential for maintaining a sense of fulfillment and balance in your life. Whether it's pursuing hobbies that bring you joy, exercising to care for your physical health, learning new skills or knowledge to expand your horizons, or spending quality time with loved ones to nurture relationships, these activities can contribute positively to your overall well-being.

By focusing on activities that resonate with your aspirations and values, you can cultivate a sense of purpose and satisfaction in your daily life. Prioritizing self-care and personal growth through such activities can also help you manage stress, improve your mood, and enhance your overall quality of life.

Remember to carve out time in your schedule for activities that bring you fulfillment and joy. Listen to your inner voice, honor your values, and make choices that support your well-being and long-term goals. By investing in yourself through meaningful activities, you can lead a more balanced, fulfilling, and purpose-driven life.

Prioritizing meaningful activities involves identifying what is most important to you and aligning your choices with those values. Here are some steps to help you prioritize meaningful activities:

1. **Identify your values: ** Reflect on what truly matters to you. What brings you joy, fulfillment, and a sense of purpose?

2. **Set clear goals: ** Define specific, achievable goals that align with your values. This will help you focus on what activities will move you closer to those goals.

3. **Evaluate your current commitments: ** Take a look at your current commitments and activities. Determine which ones align with your values and goals, and which ones may need to be adjusted or let go of.

4. **Use a priority matrix: ** Consider using tools like the Eisenhower Matrix to categorize tasks based on their importance and urgency. This can help you allocate your time and energy effectively.

5. **Practice time management: ** Manage your time wisely by setting boundaries, delegating tasks, and scheduling dedicated time for activities that align with your values.

6. **Learn to say no: ** Don't be afraid to say no to activities or commitments that do not align with your values or goals. Prioritize your well-being and focus on what truly matters to you.

7. **Reflect and adjust: ** Regularly review your priorities, goals, and activities. Adjust as

needed to ensure you are consistently focusing on meaningful activities.

Remember, prioritizing meaningful activities is a personal journey, and it may take time to find the right balance. Be patient with yourself and celebrate the progress you make towards living a more purposeful and fulfilling life.

4.4. Create a schedule: Plan your day in advance and allocate time for both productive and leisure activities. Having a structured routine can help reduce idle time spent on social media.

Creating a schedule involves the following steps:

1. **Identify your tasks and commitments**: Make a list of all the tasks you need to accomplish and any appointments or commitments you have.

2. **Prioritize tasks**: Determine which tasks are most important or time-sensitive.

3. **Allocate time blocks**: Assign specific time blocks to each task on your list. Be realistic about how much time each task will take.

4. **Include breaks**: Remember to schedule short breaks between tasks to rest and recharge.

5. **Be flexible**: Things don't always go as planned, so allow for some flexibility in your schedule to accommodate unexpected events or delays.

6. **Review and adjust**: Regularly review your schedule to see if you're staying on track and adjust as needed.

7. **Use tools**: Consider using tools like calendars, planners, or apps to help you stay organized and on top of your schedule.

4.5. Practice mindfulness: Be aware of how much time you spend on these activities and how they make you feel. Mindful awareness can help you make conscious choices about where to allocate your time and energy.

4.6. Remove distractions: Keep your phone out of sight, disable notifications, or use website blockers to minimize temptations and make it easier to focus on more important tasks.

Removing distractions can be done by implementing the following tips:

1. **Identify the distractions**: Recognize what distracts you the most so you can address them directly.

2. **Create a conducive workspace**: Set up a clean and organized workspace free from unnecessary items.

3. **Establish a routine**: Create a schedule and stick to it to maintain focus.

4. **Use productivity tools**: Utilize apps or tools that block distracting websites or help you stay focused.

5. **Take breaks**: Regular breaks can help refresh your mind and improve focus.

6. **Practice mindfulness**: Train your mind to be present and focused on the task at hand.

7. **Set goals**: Clearly defined goals can help keep you motivated and on track.

8. **Communicate your needs**: Let others know when you need time to focus without interruptions.

9. **Limit multitasking**: Focus on one task at a time to avoid getting overwhelmed by multiple distractions.

10. **Take care of yourself**: Ensure you are well-rested, hydrated, and nourished as physical well-being can impact your ability to focus.

4.7. Seek alternative sources of fulfillment: Explore activities that bring you joy, fulfillment, and a sense of accomplishment. This could include volunteering, pursuing a hobby, or investing in personal development.

Seeking alternative sources of fulfillment can be a valuable journey towards personal growth and well-being. Here are some steps you can consider taking:

4.7.1. **Self-Reflection**: Start by reflecting on what truly brings you fulfillment and joy. Identify activities, hobbies, or relationships that make you feel happy and fulfilled.

4.7.2. **Explore New Interests**: Engage in new activities or hobbies that challenge you and pique your curiosity. This could be joining a class, trying a new sport, exploring creative pursuits, or volunteering for a cause you care about.

4.7.3. **Cultivate Relationships**: Build and nurture meaningful relationships with friends, family, or community members. Surrounding yourself with positive and supportive people can greatly enhance your sense of fulfillment.

4.7.4. **Practice Gratitude**: Take time to appreciate the small things in life and acknowledge the positive aspects of your daily experiences. Gratitude can shift your perspective and help you find fulfillment in moments that may otherwise go unnoticed.

4.7.5. **Set Meaningful Goals**: Establish personal goals that align with your values and aspirations. Working towards these goals can give you a sense of purpose and fulfillment as you make progress and achieve milestones.

4.7.6. **Mindfulness and Meditation**: Incorporate mindfulness practices or meditation into your daily routine to help you become more present and aware of your thoughts and emotions. This can lead to a deeper sense of fulfillment and contentment.

4.7.7. **Engage in Self-Care**: Prioritize self-care activities that nourish your body, mind, and spirit. This could include exercise, healthy eating, adequate sleep, spending time in nature, or practicing relaxation techniques.

4.7.8. **Seek Professional Help**: If you're struggling to find fulfillment or experiencing emotional challenges that impact your well-being, consider seeking support from a therapist or counselor. They can help you explore underlying issues and develop strategies to enhance your sense of fulfillment.

"Remember, the journey to finding alternative sources of fulfillment is unique to each individual. Be open to exploring different paths, stay curious, and prioritize activities that resonate with your values and bring you a sense of joy and purpose."

5. Invest in personal growth:

Take up new hobbies, learn new skills, or work on improving yourself in areas of interest.

Investing in personal growth can have numerous benefits, such as increasing your self-confidence, expanding your knowledge and perspective, enhancing your creativity, and improving your overall well-being. It can also open up new opportunities and help you reach your full potential in various aspects of life. By continuously learning and developing yourself, you can adapt to changes more effectively and lead a more fulfilling and enriched life.

Investing in personal growth also involves setting goals, both short-term and long-term, and actively working towards achieving them. This process can help you stay motivated and focused on your personal development journey. Additionally, surrounding yourself with supportive and like-minded individuals who encourage and inspire you can further fuel your growth.

Taking time for self-reflection, meditation, or journaling can also be beneficial in gaining insight into your values, beliefs, and aspirations. This self-awareness can guide you in making meaningful decisions and taking purposeful actions that align with your personal growth objectives.

Ultimately, investing in personal growth is a lifelong journey that requires dedication, patience, and a willingness to step out of your comfort zone. Embracing challenges, embracing failures as learning opportunities, and celebrating your successes along the way are all integral parts of this transformative process. By prioritizing your personal growth and development, you can cultivate a more fulfilling and purposeful life while fulfilling your true potential.

Investing in personal growth is crucial for achieving success and fulfillment in various aspects of life. Here are some effective ways to invest in your personal growth:

1. **Setting Goals**: Define your short-term and long-term goals to give you direction and motivation. Make sure your goals are specific, measurable, attainable, relevant, and time-bound (SMART).

Short-term goal:
To further refine my conversational abilities by engaging in more structured interactions with users and improving my response generation to be more accurate and relevant. I aim to achieve this goal within the next three months by analyzing user feedback regularly and incorporating improvements into my responses.

Long-term goal:
To expand my knowledge across a wider range of topics and improve my ability to provide in-depth and insightful answers to user queries. I

plan to achieve this goal within the next year by continuously learning from user interactions, undergoing regular updates to my training data, and incorporating advanced techniques to enhance my understanding and responses.

2. **Continuous Learning**: Never stop learning. Read books, take courses, attend workshops, and seek out mentors to expand your knowledge and skills in areas that interest you.

Always keep your mind open to new experiences, stay curious, and be willing to challenge yourself. Learning is a lifelong journey that can lead to personal growth and fulfillment. Embrace opportunities to learn from diverse sources, and remember that there is always something new to discover.

Seek out knowledge in various domains, such as technology, art, history, science, and philosophy, to gain a broad perspective on the world. Engage with different viewpoints and perspectives to expand your understanding and enrich your thinking. Remember that learning is not just about acquiring information, but also about building critical thinking skills and fostering creativity. Stay motivated, stay curious, and never stop exploring the wonders of the world through continuous learning.

Continuous learning is a lifelong process of acquiring new knowledge, skills, and experiences to adapt to changing circumstances and improve oneself personally and professionally. Here are some ways to engage in continuous learning:

1. **Set learning goals: ** Define what you want to learn and why it's important to you.

2. **Stay curious: ** Be open to new ideas, perspectives, and experiences.

3. **Read widely: ** Explore books, articles, and research in various fields of interest.

4. **Take courses: ** Enroll in online courses, workshops, or classes to learn new skills.

5. **Network: ** Connect with people who have different backgrounds and expertise to learn from their experiences.

6. **Reflect on your learning: ** Regularly assess your progress and make adjustments to maximize your learning.

Remember, continuous learning is about embracing the opportunity for growth and development throughout your life.

3. **Self-Reflection**: Regularly reflect on your thoughts, emotions, and actions to gain insight into yourself and your motivations. This can help you identify areas for improvement.

Regular self-reflection is indeed a valuable practice that can lead to personal growth and self-awareness. By taking the time to reflect on our thoughts, emotions, and actions, we can gain deeper insights into ourselves, understand our motivations better, and identify areas where we can improve.

Self-reflection allows us to pause and evaluate our beliefs, values, and priorities. It helps us understand our reactions to different situations and why we may be feeling a certain way. This awareness can lead to more conscious decision-making and behavior, as we become more attuned to our true selves.

Moreover, by regularly reflecting on our thoughts, emotions, and actions, we can track our progress, set personal goals, and work towards becoming the best version of ourselves. It's a practice that promotes mindfulness, emotional intelligence, and personal development.

In conclusion, by incorporating regular self-reflection into our routines, we can gain invaluable insights into ourselves, cultivate self-awareness, and ultimately lead more fulfilling and authentic lives.

Self-reflection is a multifaceted process that involves introspection, observation, and honest assessment. It requires us to examine our thoughts, feelings, and behaviors with openness and curiosity. Through this practice, we start to uncover patterns in our thinking, identify our strengths and weaknesses, and gain a deeper understanding of ourselves.

Self-reflection can take many forms, including journaling, meditation, discussions with trusted friends or mentors, or simply taking time to pause and contemplate our experiences. It's not always easy to confront our vulnerabilities or acknowledge areas where we may fall short, but doing so is a crucial part of personal growth.

By reflecting on our thoughts, emotions, and actions, we can also enhance our relationships with others. Developing a better understanding of ourselves allows us to communicate more effectively, empathize with others, and build stronger connections based on authenticity and self-awareness.

Ultimately, self-reflection is a journey of self-discovery and self-improvement. It empowers us to learn from our past experiences, make informed choices in the present, and shape our future in alignment with our values and aspirations. It is a powerful tool for personal development and cultivating a more fulfilling and purposeful life.

4. **Step Out of Your Comfort Zone**: Growth happens when you step out of your comfort zone and take on challenges that push you to learn and adapt. Embrace new experiences and opportunities for growth.

Embracing new experiences and opportunities for growth can help you expand your horizons, develop new skills, and gain valuable insights. It may feel daunting to step out of your comfort zone, but that's where real growth happens. Being open to challenges and pushing yourself beyond what you already know can lead to personal development and a deeper understanding of yourself and the world around you. So, don't be afraid to take risks, try new things, and embrace the unknown. That's where the magic truly lies.

Stepping out of your comfort zone can be a challenging but rewarding experience. Here are some steps that can help you do so:

1. **Identify your comfort zone: ** Understand what your comfort zone looks like and the areas where you tend to stay within familiar boundaries.

2. **Set clear goals: ** Define what you want to achieve by stepping out of your comfort zone. Having a clear goal can motivate you to take action.

3. **Start small: ** Begin by taking small steps outside of your comfort zone. Gradually increase the level of challenge as you become more comfortable with discomfort.

4. **Embrace fear and uncertainty: ** Acknowledge that stepping out of your comfort zone can be scary and uncomfortable. Embrace the fear and use it as a catalyst for growth.

5. **Challenge negative thoughts: ** Identify any limiting beliefs or negative thoughts that are holding you back. Challenge these thoughts and replace them with positive affirmations.

6. **Try new things: ** Explore new activities, hobbies, or experiences that push you beyond your boundaries. This can help you build confidence and resilience.

7. **Seek support: ** Surround yourself with supportive friends, family members, or mentors

who can encourage you to step out of your comfort zone.

8. **Reflect on your experiences: ** Take time to reflect on your experiences outside of your comfort zone. What did you learn? How did you grow? Use this feedback to guide your future actions.

Remember that growth and personal development often occur outside of your comfort zone. By taking proactive steps to challenge yourself, you can expand your horizons and reach new heights in both your personal and professional life.

5. **Healthy Habits**: Take care of your physical and mental well-being by adopting healthy habits such as exercising regularly, eating nutritious foods, getting enough sleep, and managing stress.

These habits can help you maintain a healthy lifestyle and improve your overall well-being.

Regular exercise not only keeps your body strong and fit but also improves your mental health by reducing stress and anxiety. Eating nutritious foods provides your body with essential nutrients that support your physical and mental functions. Getting enough sleep is crucial for your body to rest and recharge, allowing you to be more focused and productive during the day. Finally, managing stress through relaxation techniques, mindfulness, or hobbies can help you maintain a positive mindset and cope with life's challenges more effectively. Remember, taking care of yourself is essential for leading a happy and fulfilling life.

It's important to listen to your body and mind's needs, understanding that self-care is not selfish but necessary for overall well-being. Prioritize self-care by setting boundaries, saying no when needed, and seeking support when feeling overwhelmed. Engage in activities that bring you joy and relaxation, such as spending time in nature, practicing mindfulness, or pursuing hobbies. Remember to be kind to yourself, celebrate your accomplishments, and practice self-compassion. Taking care of your physical and mental health is an ongoing journey, so be patient with yourself and make small, consistent efforts towards a healthier and happier you.

Developing healthy habits involves making small, consistent changes to your daily routine that promote overall well-being. Here are some tips to help you create and maintain healthy habits:

1. Set specific and realistic goals: Define clear objectives for what you want to achieve with your healthy habits.

2. Start small: Focus on making one or two changes at a time to avoid feeling overwhelmed.

3. Be consistent: Stick to your new habits daily to help make them a regular part of your routine.

4. Stay accountable: Share your goals with a friend or family member to help keep you on track.

5. Prioritize self-care: Make time for activities that help reduce stress and promote mental well-being, such as meditation or exercise.

6. Get enough sleep: Aim for 7-9 hours of quality sleep each night to support overall health.

7. Stay hydrated: Drink plenty of water throughout the day to keep your body functioning optimally.

8. Eat a balanced diet: Focus on consuming a variety of nutrient-rich foods to support your energy levels and overall health.

9. Stay active: Incorporate regular physical activity into your routine, whether it's going for a walk, doing yoga, or hitting the gym.

10. Continuously evaluate and adjust: Regularly assess your progress and make any necessary adjustments to ensure you are on the right track towards building and maintaining healthy habits.

6. **Networking**: Surround yourself with positive and supportive individuals who encourage your growth and push you to be your best self. Build a strong network of mentors, peers, and friends who inspire you. Surrounding yourself with positive and supportive individuals who encourage your growth and push you to be your best self is crucial for personal development and success. Building a strong network of mentors, peers, and friends who inspire you can help you stay motivated, overcome challenges, and reach your full potential.

Surrounding yourself with positive, supportive individuals can have a significant impact on your mindset, motivation, and overall well-being. Seek out people who believe in your potential, provide constructive feedback, and push you to step out of your comfort zone. By cultivating a strong network of mentors, peers, and friends who inspire you, you can create a supportive environment that nurtures your personal growth and helps you achieve your goals.

7. **Practice Mindfulness**: Cultivate mindfulness through practices like meditation, yoga, or deep breathing exercises. Being more present can help you manage stress, improve focus, and foster self-awareness.
Cultivating mindfulness through practices like meditation, yoga, or deep breathing exercises can have numerous benefits for your mental and emotional well-being. By being more present in the moment, you can learn to manage stress more effectively, improve your

focus and concentration, and develop a greater sense of self-awareness.

Meditation is a popular practice for developing mindfulness. By sitting quietly and focusing on your breath or a specific mantra, you can train your mind to stay in the present moment and let go of distracting thoughts. Over time, regular meditation practice can help reduce anxiety and improve your ability to stay calm in stressful situations.

Yoga is another great way to cultivate mindfulness while also improving your physical health. Through a series of poses and breathing exercises, yoga can help you become more aware of your body and mind, as well as improve your flexibility, strength, and balance.

Deep breathing exercises are simple techniques that can be practiced anywhere, anytime to promote relaxation and mindfulness. By taking slow, deep breaths and focusing on the sensations of each inhale and exhale, you can calm your nervous system, reduce tension, and bring your attention back to the present moment.

Overall, incorporating mindfulness practices into your daily routine can have a profound impact on your overall well-being, helping you to navigate life's challenges with greater ease and resilience.

Practicing mindfulness through meditation, yoga, or deep breathing exercises can lead to improved emotional regulation, enhanced self-awareness, and increased resilience in the face of adversity. Consistent engagement in these practices can help you develop a deeper connection to yourself and the world around you, leading to a greater sense of peace and fulfillment in your daily life. By making mindfulness a priority, you can cultivate a more balanced and centered approach to navigating the complexities of our modern world.

8. **Seek Feedback**: Be open to receiving feedback from others and use it constructively to identify areas for improvement. Feedback can provide valuable insights and help you grow.

Being open to receiving feedback from others is crucial for personal and professional growth. Constructive feedback allows you to see things from different perspectives, identify blind spots, and recognize areas where you can improve. While receiving feedback may sometimes be challenging, it is important to approach it with an open mind and a willingness to learn and grow. By incorporating feedback into your self-improvement efforts, you can continuously develop and reach your full potential. Remember, feedback is a gift that can help you become the best version of yourself.

Seeking feedback is an important skill that can help you improve and grow. Here are some tips on how to seek feedback effectively:

1. Be specific: Ask for feedback on a particular aspect, project, or skill that you want to improve. Specific questions will help you get more targeted and actionable feedback.

2. Choose the right person: Seek feedback from someone who is knowledgeable and experienced in the area you want feedback on. It could be a mentor, a peer, a manager, or a subject matter expert.

3. Be open-minded: Approach feedback with an open mind and a willingness to learn and grow. Remember that feedback is meant to help you improve, not criticize you.

4. Ask for both positive and constructive feedback: Ask for both what you did well and what you can improve on. Positive feedback can help reinforce your strengths, while constructive feedback can highlight areas for improvement.

5. Act on the feedback: Once you receive feedback, take the time to reflect on it and consider how you can apply it to improve your work or skills.

6. Express gratitude: Remember to thank the person who provided you with feedback, regardless of whether it was positive or constructive. Show that you value their input.

7. Follow up: If you receive feedback on making improvements, follow up with the person who provided the feedback to let them know how you have applied it and what changes you have made.

By following these tips, you can seek feedback effectively and use it to enhance your performance and development.

9. **Take Action**: Put your ideas into action and don't be afraid to make mistakes along the way. Failure is a natural part of growth and can provide valuable lessons for future success.

Taking action and stepping out of your comfort zone can lead to amazing opportunities and personal growth. Embrace the possibility of making mistakes, as they are essential stepping stones towards success. Learn from each failure, adjust your approach, and keep moving forward with determination and a growth mindset. Celebrate your progress and stay resilient in the face of challenges, as every mistake brings you closer to achieving your goals.

Embrace the process of turning your ideas into reality. Don't let fear of failure hold you back from taking the necessary steps towards your goals. Remember that mistakes are valuable opportunities for learning and growth. Stay proactive, persistent, and open-minded as you navigate the challenges along the way. Each step forward, no matter how small, brings you closer to realizing your aspirations. Keep pushing forward, and trust in your ability to learn and adapt as you progress towards success.

10. **Celebrate Your Wins**: Acknowledge and celebrate your achievements, no matter how small. Recognizing your progress can boost your confidence and motivation to continue investing in your personal growth.

It's important to acknowledge and celebrate your wins, no matter how big or small they may be. Celebrating your successes can help boost your confidence, motivation, and overall well-being. So, take the time to recognize and appreciate your accomplishments, no matter how small they may seem. You deserve to celebrate your wins!

Celebrating your wins is an important aspect of acknowledging your achievements and boosting your confidence. Here are some ways you can celebrate your wins:

1. **Acknowledge your accomplishment**: Take a moment to recognize and appreciate the effort you put into achieving your goal.

2. **Reward yourself**: Treat yourself to something you enjoy, whether it's a favorite meal, a relaxing day off, a small gift, or a fun activity.

3. **Share your success**: Celebrate with your friends, family, or colleagues. Share the good news and bask in their support and congratulations.

4. **Reflect on your journey**: Take some time to reflect on the steps you took to achieve your goal, the challenges you overcame, and the progress you've made.

5. **Set new goals**: Use your win as motivation to set new, challenging goals for yourself. Celebrating your wins can inspire you to aim higher and continue growing.

6. **Document your success**: Keep a journal or create a scrapbook to document your achievements. It can be empowering to look

back on your successes during times of self-doubt.

7. **Celebrate in your own way**: Everyone has different preferences for celebrating. Find what makes you happy and celebrate in a way that feels meaningful to you.

"Remember, personal growth is a continuous journey that requires dedication, self-awareness, and a willingness to step outside your comfort zone. By investing in yourself, you can unlock your full potential and create a fulfilling and successful life."

6. Surround yourself with positive influences:

Spend time with people who support and encourage you.

Positive influences can greatly impact your mindset, motivation, and overall well-being. Surrounding yourself with positive people, uplifting content, and environments that promote growth and positivity can help you stay motivated, focused, and inspired. Seek out individuals who support and encourage you, engage in activities that bring you joy, and consume media that uplifts and motivates you. By surrounding yourself with positivity, you can cultivate a more optimistic outlook on life and navigate challenges with resilience and determination.

Surrounding yourself with positive influences is like creating a shield of positivity around you. When you are surrounded by people who uplift you, motivate you, and support you, you are more likely to adopt their positive mindset and energy. Positive influences can come from various sources - friends, family, mentors, inspirational books, podcasts, or even affirmations. By consciously choosing to immerse yourself in environments that exude positive vibes and surround yourself with people who radiate positivity, you are actively shaping your own mindset and emotions.

Moreover, positive influences not only help in boosting your morale and motivation but also contribute to your personal growth and development. When you interact with individuals who have a growth mindset, who believe in your potential, and who challenge you to be the best version of yourself, you tend to push your own boundaries and strive for success. Additionally, consuming positive and uplifting content can inspire you, provide you with new perspectives, and fuel your creativity.

In a world filled with various stressors, challenges, and uncertainties, having a strong support system of positive influences can act as a cornerstone of your well-being. These influences can serve as your guiding light during tough times, reminding you of your strengths, helping you stay grounded, and encouraging you to keep moving forward. So, take a moment to reflect on the influences in your life and make a conscious effort to surround yourself with positivity, for it can truly make a world of difference in your journey toward happiness and success.

Having supportive and positive influences can provide a sense of stability and motivation, helping you navigate the challenges that come your way. Surrounding yourself with people who uplift and encourage you can enhance your resilience and mental well-being. By fostering these relationships and prioritizing positivity, you can create a nurturing environment that fuels your personal growth and happiness. Remember, cultivating a strong support system is not just beneficial for your present well-being but also crucial for building a fulfilling and successful future. Cherish those positive influences and allow them to guide you through life's ups and downs.

Surrounding yourself with positive influences is essential for your mental and emotional well-being. Here are some strategies to help you achieve this:

6.1. **Evaluate Your Current Circle**: Start by evaluating the people you currently spend most of your time with. Are they positive, supportive, and uplifting? Or do they tend to bring you down with negativity and drama?
It's important to regularly evaluate the people we spend time with to ensure they are positive, supportive, and uplifting.

Surrounding oneself with encouraging and constructive individuals can greatly impact one's well-being and growth. If the current circle consists of people who bring negativity and drama, it may be beneficial to reevaluate the relationships and consider seeking out a more positive support system.

Evaluating the dynamics of our social circle involves reflecting on how each individual contributes to our life. Positive and supportive relationships can boost our self-esteem, motivate us to pursue goals, and provide comfort during challenging times. On the other hand, negative and toxic relationships can drain our energy, increase stress, and hinder personal development.

It can be helpful to consider how spending time with each person in our circle makes us feel. Do they inspire us to be our best selves, listen compassionately, and offer constructive advice? Or do they constantly criticize, create unnecessary drama, and bring negativity into our lives?

If there are individuals who consistently bring us down or do not align with our values and goals, it may be time to reassess those relationships. Surrounding ourselves with positivity and encouragement can amplify our happiness and overall well-being. Strive to nurture connections that empower and uplift you, as the quality of your relationships can greatly influence your mental and emotional health.

6.2. **Set Boundaries**: Learn to set boundaries with people who are negative or toxic. It's okay to limit your interactions with individuals who drain your energy and focus on those who uplift you.

6.3. **Seek Out Positive People**: Actively seek out individuals who radiate positivity, support you, and inspire you. Join clubs, groups, or activities where you can meet like-minded individuals who share your values and goals.

6.4. **Engage in Positive Activities**: Surround yourself with positivity by engaging in activities that bring you joy and fulfillment. This could be hobbies, sports, volunteering, or anything else that makes you happy.

6.5. **Practice Gratitude**: Cultivating an attitude of gratitude can help you focus on the positive aspects of your life and attract positivity. Reflect on the good things in your life and express appreciation for them.

6.6. **Limit Exposure to Negativity**: Be mindful of the media you consume, the conversations you engage in, and the environments you frequent. Limit exposure to negativity, whether it's from news outlets, social media, or negative individuals.

6.7. **Work on Self-Confidence**: Building your own self-confidence and self-esteem can also help you surround yourself with positive influences. When you believe in yourself, you are better able to seek out and maintain positive relationships.

6.8. **Be a Positive Influence Yourself**: Remember that you can also be a positive influence on others. Be kind, supportive, and compassionate towards others, and you are likely to attract the same energy in return.

"By implementing these strategies, you can create a more positive and uplifting environment for yourself, which can have a significant impact on your overall well-being."

7. Practice mindfulness:

Stay present in the moment and cultivate self-awareness through mindfulness practices.

Practicing mindfulness involves paying attention to the present moment without judgment. It can help you become more self-aware, reduce stress, and improve your overall well-being. Here are some tips to help you practice mindfulness:

7.1. **Focus on Your Breath**: Take a few moments to focus on your breathing. Notice the sensation of the air entering and leaving your body.

As you focus on your breath, observe the rise and fall of your chest or abdomen with each inhale and exhale. Feel the air moving in and out of your nostrils or mouth. Take slow, deep breaths, and allow yourself to relax with each breath you take. Let go of any racing thoughts and simply be present in this moment with your breath.

As you continue focusing on your breath, you may start to feel a sense of calm and relaxation washing over you. Allow yourself to fully immerse in this simple act of breathing, letting go of any distractions or worries. Each breath you take can serve as a moment of mindfulness, grounding you in the present and bringing a sense of peace to both your body and mind.

Continue focusing on your breath, noticing the rise and fall of your chest or the sensation of air entering and leaving your nostrils. With each breath, let go of any tension or stress you may be holding onto, allowing yourself to relax more deeply. Remember, the breath is always there as an anchor, guiding you back to the present moment whenever your mind starts to wander.

Close your eyes if it helps you to more fully engage with your breath. Feel the cool air as you inhale, filling your lungs and bringing a sense of clarity. Then, feel the warm air as you exhale, releasing any tension or negativity with each breath out. Notice how your body naturally knows how to breathe, how to sustain you without any conscious effort on your part.

As you breathe deeply and intentionally, you may begin to notice a sense of expansion in your chest and abdomen. Allow this feeling of expansion to fill you with a sense of openness and tranquility. Embrace this moment of stillness, where nothing else matters except the rhythm of your breath.

Remember, this simple act of focusing on your breath can be a powerful tool for finding peace and centering yourself in the midst of life's chaos. Take this time to nurture your inner calm and rejuvenate your spirit.

7.2. **Body Scan**: Close your eyes and bring your awareness to different parts of your body, starting from your toes and moving up to your head. Notice any sensations or tension you may be holding.

Next, as you bring your awareness to each part of your body, take a deep breath in and exhale slowly, imagining the tension melting away with each breath. Allow yourself to fully relax and release any stress or negative energy you may be holding onto. Take your time moving through each part of your body, and remember to breathe deeply throughout the process.

As you scan through your body, notice the sensations in each area without judgment. If you encounter any areas of tension or discomfort, breathe into those spaces and imagine them softening with each breath. Allow yourself to fully surrender and let go of any lingering stress or worry. Feel the connection between your mind and body as you bring awareness to each part, nurturing a sense of calm and relaxation throughout your being. Embrace this moment of mindfulness and self-care, honoring the sacred journey of reconnecting with yourself.

Feel the peace that comes with being present in your body and mind. Allow yourself to release any tension or negativity that you may be holding onto. With each mindful breath, feel a sense of lightness and ease washing over you. Let go of any weight you may have been carrying and allow yourself to simply be in this moment. Embrace the stillness and tranquility within you, knowing that you have the power to create space for healing and renewal. Trust in your ability to find peace and contentment through the practice of mindfulness and self-care. Embrace the journey of reconnecting with yourself and nurturing a deeper sense of well-being. In this moment, you are whole, you are present, and you are at peace.

As you continue to breathe deeply and mindfully, feel a wave of relaxation spreading throughout your body. Imagine each inhale filling you with positive energy and each exhale releasing any remaining tension or worries. Allow yourself to sink deeper into a state of calm and serenity, letting go of any distractions or noise in your mind. Embrace the stillness within you and let it envelop you in a warm, comforting embrace.

With each breath, feel a sense of peace washing over you, bringing clarity and grounding to your thoughts and emotions. Notice how each part of your body responds to this gentle practice of self-care and mindfulness. Feel the subtle shifts in energy and sensation as you bring awareness to each area, allowing yourself to fully let go and surrender to the present moment.

As you continue to nurture this connection between your mind and body, feel a profound sense of unity and wholeness washing over you. Embrace the sacred journey of self-discovery and self-compassion, honoring the unique wisdom and beauty within you. Allow yourself to be fully present, fully alive in this moment of mindfulness and relaxation. Let this experience guide you towards a greater sense of well-being and inner peace.

7.3. **Mindful Eating**: When you eat, try to pay attention to the colors, textures, and flavors of your food. Take your time to chew slowly and savor each bite.

Mindful eating is a practice that involves being fully present and aware while eating. It means paying attention to the taste, texture, and experience of eating without distractions. By practicing mindful eating, you can cultivate a healthier relationship with food, improve digestion, and become more in tune with your body's hunger and fullness cues. This approach encourages you to savor your food, eat more slowly, and appreciate the nourishment and pleasure that comes from each meal. Overall, mindful eating can help you make healthier food choices and enjoy a more satisfying and balanced diet.

Mindful eating can help you appreciate your food more, improve digestion, and help you listen to your body's hunger and fullness cues. It can also prevent overeating and promote a healthier relationship with food.

Incorporating mindful eating practices into your daily routine can also enhance your overall well-being by promoting a sense of calm and relaxation during meal times. It can increase your awareness of food choices, improve your satisfaction with meals, and reduce mindless snacking or emotional eating. By being fully present and engaged with your food, you can nourish your body and mind in a more intentional and fulfilling way.

In addition to being present and attentive while eating, mindful eating also involves listening to your body's signals and cues. This means being aware of your hunger and fullness levels, as well as any emotions or triggers that may influence, you're eating habits. By tuning into these cues, you can make more conscious decisions about when, what, and how much to eat.

Mindful eating also encourages a non-judgmental attitude towards food and eating. Instead of labeling foods as "good" or "bad," mindful eating teaches you to approach food with a sense of curiosity and compassion. This can help you break free from restrictive diets and negative thought patterns around food, leading to a more positive and balanced relationship with eating.

Practicing mindful eating can be beneficial for improving overall health and well-being. It can help prevent overeating, reduce stress around mealtime, and promote a greater sense of satisfaction and enjoyment from your meals. By incorporating mindful eating into your daily routine, you can foster a deeper connection with your body, food, and the experience of eating.

7.4. **Observing Thoughts and Emotions**: Instead of getting caught up in your thoughts and emotions, try to observe them without judgment. This can help you develop a greater sense of self-awareness.

Observing your thoughts and emotions without judgment can help you cultivate self-awareness and gain a better understanding of yourself. By stepping back and simply observing them as they arise, you can begin to recognize patterns, triggers, and underlying beliefs that influence your feelings and actions. This practice can also lead to better emotional regulation and decision-making as you become more in tune with your inner world.

When you observe your thoughts and emotions without judgment, you create a space between yourself and your reactions. This allows you to respond more intentionally rather than reactively to situations. By practicing this mindful observation, you can gain insight into the root causes of your thoughts and emotions, enabling you to address them more effectively. This self-awareness can lead to personal growth, improved relationships, and increased emotional well-being.

Observing thoughts and emotions involves being aware of your mental processes without judgment. Start by taking a few deep breaths to center yourself. Then, pay attention to your thoughts and emotions as they arise, without trying to change them. Simply observe them as if you were an outsider looking in. Notice the patterns, triggers, and reactions without getting caught up in them. Practicing mindfulness meditation can help develop this skill over time. Remember that the goal is not to suppress or control your thoughts and emotions, but to become more aware of them and how they influence your behavior.

Observing your thoughts and emotions is a powerful practice that can help you become more self-aware and manage stress effectively. As you continue to observe your inner experiences, you may start to notice recurring patterns or triggers that influence your mood and behavior. By developing this awareness, you can begin to respond to situations more consciously rather than reacting impulsively.

One helpful technique is to practice mindfulness meditation regularly. Sit in a quiet place, focus on your breath, and simply observe your thoughts and emotions as they come and go. If your mind starts to wander, gently bring your attention back to the present moment. This practice can help you cultivate a non-judgmental and compassionate attitude towards yourself and your experiences.

Another strategy is to keep a journal to track your thoughts and emotions. Writing down your inner experiences can provide valuable insights into your mental and emotional patterns. You can also use journaling as a way to express and process difficult emotions, allowing you to gain clarity and perspective on your inner world.

Remember that observing your thoughts and emotions is an ongoing practice that requires patience and self-compassion. The goal is not to eliminate negative thoughts or emotions but to develop a deeper understanding of yourself and cultivate a sense of inner peace and balance. By incorporating these techniques into your daily routine, you can gradually enhance your self-awareness and emotional intelligence.

7.5. **Engage Your Senses**: Focus on what you can see, hear, smell, taste, and touch in the present moment. This can help ground you in the here and now.

Engaging your senses involves paying attention to and actively using each of your five senses: sight, hearing, taste, smell, and touch. Here are some ways to engage your senses:

1. Sight: Take time to appreciate the beauty around you, observe colors, shapes, and movements in your environment, and engage in

activities like painting, drawing, or photography.

2. Hearing: Listen to music, nature sounds, or engage in conversations with others. Pay attention to the sounds around you and try to identify different noises in your environment.

3. Taste: Experiment with different flavors and food combinations. Try new cuisines, savor your food slowly, and pay attention to the textures and tastes of what you are eating.

4. Smell: Light scented candles, explore different fragrances, or spend time in nature where you can breathe in the fresh air and smell the flowers. Engage in aromatherapy to relax and invigorate your senses.

5. Touch: Focus on the sensations of touch by feeling different textures, such as soft fabrics, rough surfaces, or cool materials. Practice activities that involve touch, like massage, gardening, or playing a musical instrument.

By actively engaging your senses, you can enhance your awareness of the world around you and bring more mindfulness and enjoyment to your daily experiences.

7.6. **Practice Gratitude**: Take a moment each day to reflect on things you're grateful for. This can help shift your focus to the positive aspects of your life.

Taking time each day to reflect on things you're grateful for can bring a sense of positivity and contentment to your life. It can help you appreciate the good things you have, no matter how big or small, and shift your focus away from negativity or stress. Gratitude practice has been shown to improve mental well-being, reduce stress, and increase overall happiness. So, take a moment each day to think about the things you're grateful for, whether it's your health, relationships, opportunities, or simple pleasures like a beautiful sunset or a good cup of coffee.

Practicing gratitude can be a powerful tool for cultivating a positive mindset and improving your overall well-being. By taking time each day to acknowledge the things you are grateful for, you can train your brain to focus on the positive aspects of your life rather than dwelling on the negative. This shift in perspective can lead to increased feelings of happiness, resilience, and contentment.

Gratitude can be expressed in many ways, from keeping a gratitude journal where you write down things you are thankful for each day to simply taking a few moments to silently reflect on your blessings. It's not about ignoring challenges or difficulties you may be facing, but about recognizing the good things that are also present in your life.

Research has shown that regularly practicing gratitude can lead to a host of benefits, including reduced stress levels, improved relationships, better physical health, and increased overall happiness. So, if you're looking to boost your mood and enhance your well-being, consider incorporating a daily gratitude practice into your routine.

Practicing gratitude involves being mindful of the things you're thankful for and expressing appreciation for them. Here are some specific ways to practice gratitude:

1. Keep a gratitude journal: Write down a few things you are grateful for each day.

2. Express thanks: Verbally express gratitude towards others for their actions or presence in your life.

3. Focus on the positive: Try to find the silver lining in challenging situations and be grateful for the lessons they provide.

4. Practice mindfulness: Be present in the moment and appreciate the small things in life.

5. Volunteer: Help those in need and be grateful for the opportunity to make a difference.

6. Practice self-care: Take care of yourself physically, mentally, and emotionally, and be thankful for the ability to do so.

7. Surround yourself with positive influences: Spend time with people who uplift you and bring positivity into your life.

By making gratitude a daily practice, you can cultivate a more positive outlook on life and enhance your overall well-being.

7.7. **Mindful Movement**: Engage in activities like yoga, tai chi, or walking meditation, where you can pay attention to your movements and bodily sensations.

Practicing mindful movement techniques like yoga, tai chi, or walking meditation can help increase awareness of the present moment. These activities encourage connection between the mind and body, promoting relaxation and reducing stress. By focusing on bodily sensations and movements, individuals can cultivate a sense of calm and improve overall well-being. Consistent engagement in mindful movement practices can also enhance flexibility, balance, and concentration. Make time for these activities to center yourself and promote a deeper connection with your body and mind.

By incorporating mindful movement into your routine, you can also improve your physical health by increasing flexibility, strength, and balance. Yoga, for example, focuses on fluid movements that help improve flexibility and build strength in different muscle groups. Tai chi emphasizes slow, deliberate movements that enhance balance and coordination. Walking meditation encourages you to be fully present in each step, fostering a sense of grounded Ness and attentiveness. These activities not only benefit your physical health but also provide mental clarity and emotional balance. Taking the time to engage in mindful movement practices can be a powerful way to care for your overall well-being and cultivate a deeper connection with yourself.

Incorporating mindful movement practices into your routine can have numerous benefits for your overall well-being. By engaging in activities like yoga, tai chi, or walking meditation, you are not only improving your physical health but also nurturing your mental and emotional well-being. Here are some ways in which these practices can enhance different aspects of your life:

1. Physical Health:
   - **Flexibility**: Mindful movement practices such as yoga involve stretching and lengthening the muscles, which can improve flexibility and range of motion.
   - **Strength**: Yoga, with its focus on holding poses and bodyweight exercises, can help build muscular strength.

- **Balance**: Tai chi, in particular, emphasizes slow and deliberate movements that can enhance balance and coordination, reducing the risk of falls and improving stability as you age.

2. Mental Clarity:
   - Engaging in mindful movement allows you to focus on the present moment, which can help quiet the mind and reduce racing thoughts.
   - Moving mindfully can facilitate a meditative state, promoting relaxation and mental clarity.

3. Emotional Balance:
   - Mindful movement practices can be grounding and centering, helping you connect with your emotions and process them in a healthy way.
   - Regular practice of mindful movement can reduce stress and anxiety, promoting emotional balance and well-being.

4. Connection with Self:

- Mindful movement encourages you to listen to your body and be present in the moment, deepening your connection with yourself.
   - These practices can foster self-awareness and self-compassion, allowing you to better understand and care for your needs.

By incorporating mindful movement into your routine, you are not only taking care of your physical health but also nurturing your mental and emotional well-being. Making time for these practices can have a profound impact on your overall health and help you cultivate a deeper connection with yourself.

7.8. **Mindful Communication**: Practice listening attentively when others speak and try to respond mindfully, considering your words before you speak.

Listening attentively and responding mindfully in conversations can improve communication, build stronger relationships, and demonstrate respect for others. It involves being present in the moment, focusing on what the speaker is saying without distractions, and taking the time to understand their perspective before formulating a thoughtful response. This practice fosters deeper connections, reduces misunderstandings, and promotes empathy and understanding in our interactions with others.

Mindful communication is a valuable skill that can enhance relationships and create meaningful connections. By actively listening to others and responding thoughtfully, we demonstrate respect, empathy, and consideration in our interactions. This practice fosters mutual understanding, reduces conflicts, and strengthens connections with those around us. Being mindful in communication allows us to convey our thoughts and feelings effectively while also fostering a sense of openness, trust, and cooperation in our relationships.

"Remember that mindfulness is a skill that takes practice, so be patient with yourself as you work on cultivating self-awareness and staying present in the moment."

8. Seek professional help if needed:

If you are struggling to focus on yourself due to mental health issues, consider reaching out to a therapist or counselor for support.

If you are finding it difficult to focus on yourself because of mental health challenges, seeking help from a therapist or counselor can be extremely beneficial. They can provide you with guidance, tools, and support to work through your issues and improve your mental well-being. Remember, it's okay to ask for help when you need it. Your mental health is important, and taking steps to address it is a sign of strength.

Continuing to prioritize your mental health is important for your overall well-being. Therapy or counseling can provide a safe and supportive space for you to explore your feelings, learn coping mechanisms, and develop strategies to improve your mental health. A therapist can help you gain insight into your thoughts and behaviors, identify triggers that may be affecting your ability to focus on yourself, and work on building a healthier relationship with yourself.

Mental health issues can feel overwhelming and isolating, but seeking professional help can make a positive difference. Therapists and counselors are trained to help you navigate your emotions, manage stress, and develop self-care practices that can support your mental health journey. Remember, asking for help is a courageous step towards healing and growth. Your well-being is worth investing in, and seeking professional support can empower you to focus on yourself and create a more fulfilling life.

Seeking professional help when needed is an important step for taking care of your mental health. Here are some steps you can take to seek professional help:

1. **Acknowledge the Need: ** Recognize that you may need professional help and that it's okay to ask for it.

Acknowledging the need involves recognizing and accepting that a particular requirement or desire exists. Here are some steps to acknowledge the need effectively:

1.1. **Self-reflection**: Take time to reflect on your thoughts, feelings, and behaviors to identify areas where a need might be unmet.

1.2. **Active listening**: Pay attention to your inner thoughts and emotions, as well as feedback from others, to understand what you truly need.

1.3. **Mindfulness**: Practice being present in the moment to tune into your needs and feelings without judgment.

1.4. **Define the need**: Clearly identify and articulate what you need, whether it's emotional support, a physical resource, or anything else.

1.5. **Express your need**: Communicate your need to yourself or others in a constructive and assertive manner.

1.6. **Seek support**: Don't be afraid to ask for help or guidance when necessary to fulfill your needs.

1.7. **Self-care**: Prioritize self-care activities that address your needs, whether they are related to physical, emotional, mental, or spiritual well-being.

Remember, acknowledging your needs is a crucial step in taking care of yourself and living a more fulfilling life.

2. **Identify the Right Professional: ** Depending on your needs, you may seek help from a

therapist, counselor, psychologist, psychiatrist, or other mental health professionals.

Identifying the right professional for your needs requires careful consideration and research. Here are some tips to help you find the right professional:

2.1. Define Your Needs: Clearly define the services or expertise you require. Understanding your needs will help you narrow down the type of professional you are looking for.

2.2. Research: Look for professionals who specialize in the specific area you need help with. You can use online search engines, professional directories, or ask for recommendations from colleagues or friends.

2.3. Check Qualifications and Experience: Look for professionals who have the necessary qualifications, certifications, and experience in the field. This can help ensure that they have the expertise to meet your needs.

2.4. Read Reviews and Testimonials: Check online reviews and testimonials from previous clients to get an idea of the professional's reputation and quality of service.

2.5. Interview Multiple Professionals: Don't hesitate to reach out to multiple professionals to discuss your needs and ask questions. This can help you assess their knowledge, communication style, and how well they understand your requirements.

2.6. Consider Communication and Compatibility: Choose a professional with whom you feel comfortable communicating. Good communication is key to a successful working relationship.

2.7. Consider Cost and Budget: Compare the costs of different professionals and consider your budget before making a decision.

Remember that the cheapest option may not always be the best choice.

2.8. Trust Your Instincts: Ultimately, trust your instincts and choose a professional you feel confident in and comfortable working with.

By following these tips, you can increase your chances of finding the right professional to meet your needs.

3. **Do Your Research: ** Look for professionals who specialize in the area you need help with and who you feel comfortable with.

When conducting research, it's important to follow a systematic and organized approach to ensure accuracy and validity. Here are some steps to help you effectively conduct your research:

3.1. Identify your research question or topic: Start by clearly defining what you want to research. Formulate a specific question or topic that you want to explore.

3.2. Conduct a literature review: Search for existing information, studies, and sources related to your research question. This will help you understand what work has already been done in the area and identify gaps in the existing knowledge.

3.3. Develop a research plan: Create a detailed plan outlining your research methodology, including the research design, data collection methods, sampling strategy, and analysis techniques.

3.4. Collect data: Depending on your research question, collect data through experiments, surveys, interviews, observations, or other methods. Ensure that your data collection methods are appropriate for your research question and objectives.

3.5. Analyze data: Once you have collected your data, analyze it using appropriate statistical or qualitative analysis techniques. Interpret the results in the context of your research question.

3.6. Draw conclusions: Based on your analysis, draw conclusions that answer your research question or contribute to the existing knowledge in your field.

3.7. Write your research report: Organize your findings, methodology, analysis, and conclusions into a coherent research report. Make sure to properly cite your sources and adhere to academic writing standards.

3.8. Review and revise: Have your work reviewed by peers or mentors to get feedback on the quality and validity of your research. Revise your work based on this feedback to improve its quality.

3.9. Publish or present your research: Share your research findings through publication in academic journals, presentations at conferences, or other appropriate channels to contribute to the body of knowledge in your field.

Remember to be thorough, systematic, and critical in your approach to research to ensure the reliability and validity of your findings.

4. **Reach Out: ** Contact the professional through their office, email, or phone to schedule an appointment.

"Reaching out" typically refers to making contact or connecting with someone. Here are some general steps on how to reach out effectively:

4.1. **Identify your purpose: ** Be clear about why you are reaching out to the person or group.

4.2. **Choose the right medium: ** Decide whether to reach out via email, phone call, social media, or in person, depending on the context and your relationship with the person.

4.3. **Personalize your message: ** Tailor your communication to the recipient by addressing them by name and mentioning any shared interests or connections.

4.4. **Be concise: ** Keep your message brief and to the point, stating clearly what you are asking or discussing.

4.5. **Be polite and respectful: ** Use a friendly and professional tone in your communication.

4.6. **Follow up: ** If you don't receive a response, consider sending a follow-up message after a reasonable amount of time.

Remember that effective communication skills are key to successfully reaching out to others.

5. **Attend Appointments: ** Be open and honest with the professional during your

appointments to get the most out of the help they provide.

Attending appointments involves a few key steps:

5.1. Make sure you have all the details, such as date, time, and location.

5.2. Set reminders or alarms to ensure you don't forget.

5.3. Plan your schedule around the appointment to avoid conflicts.

5.4. Arrive on time or early to show respect for the other person's time.

5.5. Bring any necessary documents or information.

5.6. Stay engaged and present during the appointment.

5.7. Follow up as needed after the appointment.

By following these steps, you can effectively attend appointments and make the most of your time.

"Remember, it's okay to ask for help when you need it, and seeking professional help is a positive step towards improving your mental well-being."

9. Prioritize self-reflection:

Take time to reflect on your thoughts, emotions, and experiences. Journaling can be a helpful tool for self-reflection.

Self-reflection can help you gain a deeper understanding of yourself, your behaviors, and your motivations. By taking the time to reflect, you can identify patterns, areas for growth, and potential solutions to challenges you may be facing. This practice can also lead to increased self-awareness, improved decision-making, and a greater sense of overall well-being. Remember to prioritize self-reflection as part of your regular routine to promote personal growth and development.

Prioritizing self-reflection allows you to cultivate mindfulness, enhance your emotional intelligence, and build a stronger connection with yourself. It can also help you manage stress, improve relationships, and make more informed decisions in various aspects of your life. By integrating self-reflection into your daily routine, you can foster personal development and lead a more fulfilling and purposeful life.

By setting aside time for self-reflection each day, you create a space to analyze your thoughts and actions, identify areas for growth, and gain a deeper understanding of your values and beliefs. This process can help you become more self-aware, leading to better self-regulation and an improved ability to respond to challenges effectively.

Furthermore, self-reflection can enhance your relationships with others by giving you the opportunity to consider how your behavior and interactions impact those around you. Through self-awareness and introspection, you can develop empathy, understanding, and compassion, which are essential qualities for building strong and meaningful connections with others.

In addition, practicing self-reflection can boost your decision-making skills by providing clarity on your goals, priorities, and values. When you understand yourself better, you are better equipped to make choices that align with your authentic self and lead to greater satisfaction and success.

Overall, prioritizing self-reflection is a powerful tool for personal growth and well-being. By making it a consistent part of your routine, you can cultivate mindfulness, emotional intelligence, and self-awareness, leading to a more balanced, fulfilling, and purposeful life.

Certainly! Here are more benefits of prioritizing self-reflection:

1. **Enhanced Problem-Solving Skills: ** Self-reflection allows you to assess situations from multiple perspectives, leading to more creative and effective problem-solving strategies.

Self-reflection enables individuals to step back, consider various viewpoints, and approach problems with greater creativity, leading to more effective problem-solving strategies.

Here are some tips to enhance your problem-solving skills:

1. Practice critical thinking: Develop the ability to analyze situations objectively and think logically.

2. Learn from mistakes: Reflect on past experiences to understand what went wrong and how you can improve.

3. Collaborate with others: Working in teams can provide different perspectives and solutions to a problem.

4. Break down the problem: Divide a complex problem into smaller, manageable parts to tackle them one by one.

5. Be open-minded: Embrace new ideas and approaches to problem-solving, even if they challenge your current beliefs.

6. Stay organized: Keep track of your progress and maintain a structured approach to problem-solving.

7. Seek feedback: Ask for input from others to gain different insights and improve your problem-solving skills over time.

8. Think creatively: Don't limit yourself to conventional solutions. Explore unconventional and creative approaches to solving problems.

9. Develop resilience: Challenges and setbacks are part of problem-solving. Build resilience to stay motivated and persevere through difficulties.

10. Stay updated: Keep yourself informed about new technologies, trends, and advancements in

your field to apply the latest knowledge to problem-solving.

11. Practice mindfulness: Being present in the moment can help you focus better and make clearer decisions when faced with challenges.

12. Take breaks: Sometimes stepping away from a problem can give you a fresh perspective and lead to new insights or solutions.

13. Learn from others: Observe how others approach and solve problems, and incorporate successful strategies into your problem-solving toolkit.

14. Set goals: Define clear objectives and milestones to track your progress and stay on course when solving complex problems.

15. Embrace complexity: Be comfortable dealing with ambiguity and uncertainty, as complex problems often require innovative and adaptive solutions.

2. **Improved Communication: ** By understanding your thoughts and emotions, you can communicate more clearly and effectively, fostering better relationships and reducing misunderstandings.

By being more in tune with your own thoughts and emotions, you can express yourself more authentically and with greater clarity. This self-awareness helps you communicate in a way that is more genuine and considerate of others' feelings. When you are able to articulate your thoughts and emotions effectively, you can connect with others on a deeper level, leading to stronger, more meaningful relationships. Improved communication also reduces the likelihood of misunderstandings, as you are better equipped to convey your message in a way that is easily understood by others.

Understanding your thoughts and emotions can significantly enhance your communication skills. When you are aware of your own feelings and can accurately identify and express them, you are better equipped to communicate your needs, desires, and perspectives to others. This self-awareness not only helps you articulate your thoughts more clearly but also allows you to convey them in a way that resonates with those around you.

Moreover, by being attuned to your emotions, you can manage them effectively during conversations, preventing heated exchanges or misunderstandings. This emotional intelligence enables you to empathize with others, listen actively, and respond thoughtfully, fostering open and honest communication.

Additionally, when you communicate from a place of self-awareness and emotional understanding, you create a sense of authenticity and trust in your relationships. People are more likely to connect with you on a deeper level when they perceive you as genuine and empathetic.

Ultimately, improving your communication through understanding your thoughts and emotions not only strengthens your relationships but also contributes to a more harmonious and productive interaction with others.

3. **Increased Resilience: ** Regular self-reflection helps you build resilience by developing a better understanding of your strengths, weaknesses, and areas for improvement.

Increased awareness of these aspects can help you identify ways to cope with challenges more effectively and adapt to stressful situations with a positive mindset. By taking the time to reflect on your experiences, emotions, and reactions, you can cultivate a deeper sense of self-awareness and self-compassion. This, in turn, can empower you to navigate setbacks more skillfully and bounce back from adversity with greater resilience.

Additionally, regular self-reflection allows you to chart your progress, set meaningful goals, and track your growth over time. By recognizing patterns in your thoughts and behaviors, you can make informed decisions about how to approach future challenges and make positive changes in your life. Self-reflection also promotes mindfulness and emotional intelligence, enabling you to regulate your emotions, manage stress more effectively, and build strong relationships with others. Overall, integrating self-reflection into your routine can enhance your mental and emotional well-being, strengthen your resilience, and support your personal growth and development.

By dedicating time to self-reflection, you can gain valuable insights into your values, beliefs, strengths, and areas for improvement. This increased self-awareness empowers you to make choices that align with your authentic self and fosters a deeper sense of fulfillment and purpose. Moreover, reflecting on past experiences can help you learn from mistakes, extract important lessons, and adapt your behaviors and attitudes accordingly.

In addition to improving your personal life, regular self-reflection can have a positive impact on your professional endeavors. By assessing your performance, identifying areas of growth, and setting actionable goals, you can enhance your productivity, creativity, and overall effectiveness at work. Furthermore, self-reflection can aid in cultivating a growth mindset and a willingness to embrace challenges and feedback, ultimately driving continuous learning and professional development.

In essence, embracing self-reflection as a deliberate practice in your daily life holds the potential to transform your overall well-being, relationships, and success both personally and professionally. It serves as a powerful tool for self-improvement, guiding you towards a more purposeful and fulfilling existence. So, take the time to pause, reflect, and introspect regularly—it may be the key to unlocking your full potential and leading a more enriching life.

Embracing self-reflection as a regular practice can also promote greater resilience in the face of adversity. Through introspection, you can develop a deeper understanding of your reactions to challenges, setbacks, and failures. This heightened self-awareness allows you to approach obstacles with a more constructive and adaptive mindset, enabling you to bounce back more effectively from difficult situations.

Moreover, self-reflection can be a powerful tool for enhancing your decision-making skills. By reflecting on past choices and their outcomes, you can discern patterns and trends in your decision-making process. This reflective insight can help you make more informed and thoughtful decisions in the future, leading to better outcomes and a greater sense of personal agency and control over your life.

In cultivating a habit of self-reflection, you also build a foundation for personal growth and development. By continuously evaluating your goals, values, and aspirations, you can ensure that your actions are aligned with your long-term vision for yourself. This intentional self-examination encourages you to step out of your comfort zone, embrace new opportunities for learning and growth, and unlock your full potential.

Overall, the practice of self-reflection serves as a catalyst for transformation and positive change in all areas of your life. By engaging in introspective practices regularly, you can foster a deeper connection with yourself, cultivate greater resilience and decision-making skills, and propel yourself on a path of continuous growth and self-actualization. So, make self-reflection a priority in your daily routine and watch as it empowers you to thrive and flourish in all aspects of your life.

4. **Personal Empowerment: ** Self-reflection empowers you to take ownership of your actions, emotions, and decisions, leading to a greater sense of control over your life.

Self-reflection provides a pathway to self-awareness, helping you recognize patterns, strengths, and weaknesses, thereby enabling you to make more informed choices in alignment with your values and goals. It fosters personal growth and empowers you to cultivate resilience, authenticity, and emotional intelligence.
Engaging in self-reflection also enhances your problem-solving skills, interpersonal relationships, and decision-making abilities. It encourages mindfulness and deepens your understanding of yourself, leading to a more fulfilling and purposeful life. By taking the time to reflect on your thoughts, feelings, and actions, you can gain valuable insights that can guide you towards self-improvement and a greater sense of well-being.

Self-reflection allows you to understand yourself better, identify areas for growth, and make positive changes to live more authentically and purposefully.

Self-reflection is a powerful tool for personal development that allows you to pause, step back, and evaluate your experiences from a place of curiosity and openness. Through self-reflection, you can identify areas of your life that may be in need of attention or improvement. This process of introspection helps you gain clarity about your values, beliefs, and priorities, enabling you to align your actions with what truly matters to you.

Moreover, self-reflection can deepen your self-awareness by helping you recognize automatic thoughts and behaviors that may be holding you back. By acknowledging your strengths and weaknesses, you can leverage your talents and work on areas that require growth. This self-awareness can lead to increased confidence, as you become more attuned to your abilities and limitations.

In addition, self-reflection can strengthen your emotional intelligence, allowing you to better understand and manage your emotions. By tuning into your feelings and motivations, you can develop empathy for others and improve your communication skills. This heightened emotional intelligence can enhance your relationships with others and contribute to a more harmonious and fulfilling life.

Overall, self-reflection is a valuable practice that can lead to personal growth, resilience, and a deeper connection to your authentic self. By dedicating time to reflect on your experiences, thoughts, and emotions, you can cultivate greater self-awareness and make more informed choices that align with your values and goals.

5. **Better Mental Health: ** Reflecting on your experiences can promote self-compassion,

reduce negative self-talk, and increase overall psychological well-being.

Reflecting on your experiences can help you gain a better understanding of your thoughts, feelings, and behaviors. It allows you to identify patterns, triggers, and areas where you may need to make changes. This self-awareness is crucial for improving your mental health and well-being.

When you reflect on your experiences with self-compassion, you are more likely to treat yourself with kindness and understanding, rather than with harsh judgment and criticism. This can help reduce negative self-talk and cultivate a more positive relationship with yourself.

By taking the time to reflect on your experiences, you can also gain insights into your values, goals, and priorities. This can help you make more informed decisions and align your actions with what truly matters to you, leading to a greater sense of purpose and fulfillment.

Overall, reflecting on your experiences can be a powerful tool for promoting better mental health, enhancing self-awareness, fostering self-compassion, and improving your overall psychological well-being.

Reflecting on your experiences can also help you identify sources of stress or anxiety in your life. By examining past situations and your reactions to them, you can develop healthier coping mechanisms and strategies for managing difficult emotions. This can lead to a greater sense of control and resilience in the face of challenges.

Moreover, reflecting on your experiences can enhance your relationships with others. When you better understand yourself, you are more likely to communicate effectively, set boundaries, and express your needs. This can lead to more authentic and fulfilling connections with those around you.

In addition, regularly reflecting on your experiences can help you track your personal growth and progress over time. Celebrating your achievements, no matter how small, can boost your self-esteem and motivation to continue working towards your goals.

Overall, taking the time to reflect on your experiences can be a valuable tool for promoting better mental health, fostering self-awareness and self-compassion, improving relationships, and tracking personal growth.

6. **Goal Alignment: ** Self-reflection enables you to align your actions and behaviors with your long-term goals and values, facilitating personal and professional growth.

Self-reflection allows you to assess whether your current actions and behaviors are in line with your long-term goals and values. By taking time to reflect on your thoughts, emotions, and experiences, you can make adjustments to ensure that you are on the right path towards personal and professional growth.

Self-reflection helps you gain clarity on your values and priorities, identify areas for improvement, and make informed decisions that are in alignment with your goals. It can also enhance self-awareness and mindfulness, leading to increased emotional intelligence and better relationships with others. Additionally, regular self-reflection can boost confidence, resilience, and overall well-being by empowering you to take ownership of your actions and create a meaningful and fulfilling life.

In summary, self-reflection is a powerful tool that can help you understand yourself better, improve your decision-making, enhance your relationships with others, boost your confidence, and lead to a more meaningful and fulfilling life.

Certainly! Self-reflection involves looking inward, exploring your thoughts, emotions, and behaviors to gain insight into your beliefs and motivations. By taking the time to reflect on your actions and choices, you can learn from past experiences, set goals for the future, and make positive changes in your life. It's a process of self-discovery that allows you to grow personally and professionally, develop a deeper understanding of yourself, and navigate life with greater intention and clarity. Ultimately, self-reflection is a valuable practice that can contribute to your overall well-being and success in various aspects of your life.

7. **Increased Self-Awareness: ** Self-reflection helps you gain a deeper understanding of yourself, your values, beliefs, motivations, and emotions, leading to a more authentic and fulfilling life.

Increased self-awareness refers to the ability to reflect on one's thoughts, feelings, beliefs, motivations, and behaviors. It involves having a deeper understanding of oneself, including strengths, weaknesses, values, and goals. When someone has increased self-awareness, they are more mindful of their actions and reactions, leading to better decision-making, improved emotional intelligence, and enhanced personal growth. It can also help individuals to recognize their patterns of behavior and make any necessary changes to reach their full potential.

Increased self-awareness can be cultivated through various practices such as mindfulness meditation, journaling, therapy, self-reflection exercises, and seeking feedback from others. It enhances emotional intelligence, interpersonal relationships, and overall well-being. By being more in tune with oneself, individuals are better equipped to navigate life's challenges, make conscious choices, and lead a more authentic and fulfilling life.

Increased self-awareness through self-reflection can lead to personal growth, improved decision-making, better relationships, and a greater sense of fulfillment and authenticity in life.

Increased self-awareness can lead to personal growth, improved decision-making, and a deeper understanding of oneself and others. It plays a crucial role in enhancing various aspects of life, including emotional intelligence, relationships, and overall well-being. By engaging in practices that foster self-awareness, individuals can develop a stronger sense of identity, purpose, and fulfillment.

8. **Effective Leadership: ** Leaders who practice self-reflection are better able to understand their own strengths and weaknesses, communicate clearly with their team, and make informed decisions that benefit the organization as a whole.

Self-reflection allows leaders to gain valuable insights into their own behavior, attitudes, and decision-making processes. By regularly reflecting on their actions and outcomes, leaders can identify areas for improvement and growth. This introspective process also helps leaders become more self-aware, which is a key component of emotional intelligence—a trait that is crucial for effective leadership.

Moreover, self-reflection can enhance a leader's ability to communicate effectively with their team. Leaders who take the time to reflect on their communication style and its impact can adjust their approach to better connect with their team members. By being mindful of how their words and actions are perceived, leaders can foster trust, build strong relationships, and create a positive work environment.

Additionally, self-reflection enables leaders to make more informed decisions. By analyzing past successes and failures, evaluating different perspectives, and considering the potential outcomes of their choices, leaders can make decisions that are aligned with the organization's goals and values. This reflective process can help leaders anticipate challenges, navigate complex situations, and lead their team with confidence.

In summary, self-reflection is a powerful tool for leadership development. Leaders who engage in regular self-reflection are better equipped to understand themselves, communicate effectively, and make informed decisions that drive organizational success. By prioritizing self-reflection as a core aspect of their leadership practice, individuals can enhance their leadership skills and inspire their teams to achieve greater heights.

Leaders who engage in self-reflection also promote a culture of continuous learning and growth within their organization. By modeling the importance of self-assessment and personal development, leaders inspire their team members to reflect on their own performance, behaviors, and goals. This creates a culture of openness, feedback, and improvement, where employees feel empowered to learn from their experiences and strive for excellence.

Furthermore, self-reflection can help leaders manage stress and maintain a healthy work-life balance. By taking the time to pause, reflect, and recharge, leaders can gain clarity, perspective, and resilience in the face of challenges. This practice of self-care not only benefits the leader's well-being but also sets a positive example for their team members, encouraging them to prioritize their own self-care and mental health.

In conclusion, self-reflection is a foundational practice for effective leadership. It enhances self-awareness, communication skills, decision-making abilities, and fosters a culture of continuous learning and personal growth. Leaders who prioritize self-reflection are better equipped to lead with authenticity, empathy, and resilience, ultimately driving success for themselves and their organizations.

9. **Conflict Resolution: ** By reflecting on your own thoughts and feelings during conflicts, you can approach disagreements with a more open and empathetic mindset, leading to more constructive and peaceful resolutions.

Conflict resolution refers to the process of resolving disputes or disagreements between two or more parties in a peaceful and constructive manner. It involves strategies and techniques that help in addressing and managing conflicts effectively to reach a mutually agreeable solution.

Conflict resolution can take place in various settings, such as personal relationships, workplaces, communities, or international affairs. It often involves identifying the underlying issues causing the conflict, promoting open communication, active listening, understanding different perspectives, and finding common ground to reach a resolution. Some common approaches to conflict resolution include negotiation, mediation, arbitration, and collaborative problem-solving.

Effective conflict resolution can help prevent escalation of conflicts, improve relationships among parties involved, and foster a more positive and productive environment. It requires skills such as empathy, communication, problem-solving, and emotional intelligence to navigate through differences and find solutions that meet the needs and interests of all parties. Ultimately, conflict resolution is about finding peaceful and mutually beneficial ways to manage disagreements and promote harmony and understanding.

By approaching conflict with a constructive mindset and a willingness to engage in respectful dialogue, individuals and groups can work towards sustainable resolutions that address underlying concerns and build stronger relationships. Emphasizing collaboration, empathy, and a commitment to finding common ground can lead to long-lasting solutions that benefit everyone involved. Conflict resolution is a valuable skill that can transform challenges into opportunities for growth and understanding, ultimately contributing to a more harmonious and cooperative society across various settings.

Effective conflict resolution also involves establishing clear communication channels, setting ground rules for respectful engagement, and creating a safe space for all parties to express their perspectives without fear of judgment or retaliation. Encouraging active listening, acknowledging emotions, and validating concerns can help reduce tension and foster trust in the resolution process.

Furthermore, conflict resolution may require a third-party intervention, such as a neutral mediator or facilitator, to help guide the conversation, clarify misunderstandings, and assist in finding common interests. These neutral parties can provide an objective perspective, manage power imbalances, and help parties explore creative solutions that address the root causes of the conflict.

Ultimately, conflict resolution is a dynamic and ongoing process that requires patience, flexibility, and a commitment to finding win-win solutions that prioritize mutual respect and understanding. By approaching conflicts with an open mind and a willingness to engage in constructive dialogue, individuals and groups can transform adversarial relationships into opportunities for growth, learning, and positive change.

10. **Stress Management: ** Regular self-reflection can help you identify sources of stress in your life, explore coping mechanisms, and make necessary changes to reduce stress levels and improve your overall well-being.

Regular self-reflection is important for stress management as it helps identify sources of stress, explore coping strategies, and make necessary changes for reducing stress levels and improving overall well-being.

Engaging in self-reflection can provide valuable insights into the factors contributing to your stress levels. By taking the time to reflect on your thoughts, emotions, and behaviors, you can gain a deeper understanding of the root causes of your stress. This awareness is a crucial first step in developing effective coping mechanisms to better manage stress.

During self-reflection, you can also evaluate your current coping strategies and determine their effectiveness. Are you turning to healthy activities such as exercise, meditation, or spending time with loved ones to alleviate stress, or are you relying on habits that may be exacerbating the situation, such as excessive caffeine consumption or avoidance behaviors?

Furthermore, self-reflection allows you to assess your lifestyle and identify areas that may need adjustment to support better stress management. This could involve setting boundaries, prioritizing self-care activities, improving time management, or seeking professional help if needed.

By incorporating regular self-reflection into your routine, you can cultivate a greater sense of self-awareness, resilience, and empowerment in dealing with stress. Remember that self-care is a journey, and taking the time to reflect on your experiences can be a powerful tool for fostering personal growth and well-being.

11. **Improved Decision-Making: ** Self-reflection allows you to review past decisions, understand their outcomes, and learn from mistakes, leading to more informed and effective decision-making in the future.

Self-reflection also helps in identifying patterns in our decision-making process, recognizing our biases, and gaining insights into our values and goals. This deeper understanding can lead to more mindful and intentional decision-making, resulting in better outcomes and personal growth.

By taking the time to reflect on our decisions, we can develop a clearer understanding of our motivations, emotions, and thought processes that influence our choices. This introspection enables us to make adjustments, set priorities, and align our choices with our long-term objectives. Moreover, self-reflection promotes a sense of accountability and fosters a growth mindset, encouraging us to embrace challenges, learn from setbacks, and continuously improve our decision-making skills. Ultimately, the practice of self-reflection empowers us to make more conscious, strategic, and fulfilling decisions that support our personal and professional development.

Self-reflection serves as a powerful tool for personal growth and development by allowing us to identify patterns in our behavior and thought processes. By examining our past

decisions and their outcomes, we can learn
valuable lessons that inform our future choices.
This process of self-assessment helps us to
cultivate self-awareness, recognize areas for
improvement, and build a stronger sense of
self-efficacy.

Additionally, self-reflection can enhance
emotional intelligence by deepening our
understanding of our own and others'
emotions. It enables us to become more
empathetic, improve our relationships, and
communicate effectively with those around us.
By acknowledging our strengths and
weaknesses through introspection, we can
develop greater resilience, adaptability, and
interpersonal skills.

Taking the time for self-reflection also
contributes to mental well-being by providing
an opportunity for introspection and self-care.
It allows us to manage stress, reduce anxiety,
and gain perspective on our challenges and
achievements. By engaging in regular self-

reflection practices such as journaling, mindfulness, or seeking feedback from others, we can foster a sense of balance, clarity, and purpose in our lives.

In conclusion, self-reflection is a valuable habit that empowers us to live more intentionally, authentically, and meaningfully. By incorporating self-reflection into our daily routines, we can enhance our decision-making, emotional intelligence, and overall well-being, leading to a more fulfilling and purpose-driven life.

12. **Enhanced Creativity: ** Engaging in self-reflection can stimulate your creativity by encouraging you to explore new ideas, perspectives, and solutions to challenges you may face.

Self-reflection allows you to delve deep into your thoughts and emotions, enabling you to understand your personal values, beliefs, and motivations better. This deeper understanding can spark new insights and inspire innovative ideas that you may not have considered before. By examining your experiences and contemplating different viewpoints, you can broaden your creative thinking and come up with novel approaches to solving problems or pursuing your goals. Additionally, self-reflection provides a space for experimentation and risk-taking without the fear of judgment, which can foster a more creative and open mindset. Overall, integrating self-reflection into your routine can nurture your creativity and help you approach challenges with fresh perspectives and imaginative solutions.

Self-reflection also enables you to identify patterns in your thinking and behavior, allowing you to break free from mental blocks and habitual ways of approaching problems. It encourages you to question assumptions, explore possibilities, and connect seemingly unrelated ideas, fostering a more flexible and adaptive mindset. Moreover, by regularly reflecting on your experiences and learning from setbacks, you can cultivate resilience and a growth mindset that are essential for sustained creativity. Embracing self-reflection as a valuable tool for personal and professional growth can lead to a more fulfilling and innovative life journey.

Incorporating self-reflection into your routine can have numerous benefits across various aspects of your life, promoting personal growth, self-awareness, and emotional intelligence.

Self-reflection allows you to pause and examine your thoughts, feelings, and behaviors. By taking the time to reflect on your experiences and actions, you can gain a deeper understanding of yourself, your motivations, and your values. This process can help you identify patterns in your behavior, recognize areas for improvement, and make more informed decisions in the future. Additionally, self-reflection can enhance your relationships with others by fostering empathy, communication, and understanding. Overall, integrating self-reflection into your routine can lead to increased self-awareness, personal growth, and emotional intelligence, ultimately helping you live a more fulfilling and purposeful life.

Self-reflection can also be a powerful tool for managing stress and enhancing overall well-being. By regularly reflecting on your thoughts and emotions, you can develop a greater sense of self-compassion and resilience. This can help you navigate challenges and setbacks with more ease and grace. Additionally, self-reflection can provide a sense of clarity and direction, helping you set meaningful goals and prioritize what truly matters to you. It can also help you stay connected to your values and sense of purpose, which can contribute to a greater sense of fulfillment and satisfaction in your life. By incorporating self-reflection into your routine, you can cultivate a deeper sense of self-understanding and create a solid foundation for personal growth and self-improvement.

10. Practice gratitude:

Cultivate a sense of gratitude by reflecting on the positive aspects of your life and expressing thanks for them.

Practicing gratitude can help shift your perspective towards the good in your life, fostering a sense of contentment and happiness. It involves acknowledging the blessings, small or big, that you have received, such as good health, supportive relationships, or personal accomplishments. This practice can be as simple as keeping a gratitude journal, writing thank-you notes, or simply taking a moment each day to appreciate what you have. By focusing on the positives, you develop a more optimistic outlook, reduce stress, and enhance your overall well-being.

Practicing gratitude not only impacts your mental and emotional well-being but also has physical benefits. Studies have shown that individuals who regularly practice gratitude may experience improved sleep, lower levels of stress and depression, and enhanced resilience when facing challenges. By intentionally acknowledging and expressing gratitude for the good things in your life, you cultivate a more positive mindset that can help you navigate difficult situations with a sense of perspective and resilience.

Additionally, expressing gratitude towards others strengthens relationships and fosters a sense of connection and community. When you show appreciation for the people in your life, whether through kind words, gestures, or acts of kindness, you not only uplift their spirits but also deepen your bond with them. This reciprocal exchange of gratitude can create a supportive and positive environment that benefits all involved.

Incorporating gratitude into your daily routine can be a transformative practice that enhances your overall quality of life. Whether you choose to start your day with a gratitude meditation, keep a gratitude journal, or simply pause to reflect on your blessings throughout the day, cultivating a sense of gratitude can bring about profound shifts in your mindset and outlook. Embracing an attitude of gratitude is a powerful tool for personal growth, happiness, and well-being.

Practicing gratitude is a wonderful way to improve your overall well-being and mindset. Here are some ways you can practice gratitude:

1. Keep a gratitude journal: Take a few minutes each day to write down things you are grateful for. It can be as simple as a beautiful sunrise or a kind gesture from a friend.

Continuing to write in a gratitude journal can help cultivate a positive mindset and increase feelings of happiness and well-being. It can also serve as a reminder of the good things in your life, even during challenging times.
By

The practice of gratitude journaling is a powerful tool for shifting your focus towards the positive aspects of your life. By taking time to reflect on and write down the things you are grateful for each day, you train your mind to notice and appreciate the good things, big or small. This can lead to increased feelings of contentment, reduced stress, and improved overall mental well-being. So, grab a notebook or open a digital document, and start jotting down those moments of gratitude each day. Over time, you may be surprised at how this simple practice can positively impact your outlook on life.

2. Express appreciation: Take time to thank people in your life for their support, kindness, or help. Show genuine appreciation for the little things.

Expressing appreciation is a powerful way to strengthen relationships and spread positivity. Thanking people in your life for their support, kindness, or help can make a big impact.

Taking the time to show genuine gratitude for the little things can make someone's day brighter and strengthen the bond between you. Remember to express appreciation not just for grand gestures, but also for the small acts of kindness that often go unnoticed. Kind words and gestures of thanks can go a long way in making others feel valued and appreciated.

Here are some ways you can express appreciation in your daily interactions:

1. **Say Thank You**: A simple "thank you" can go a long way in showing appreciation for someone's actions or words. Whether it's holding the door open for you, helping you with a task, or simply being there for you, acknowledging their efforts with a heartfelt thank you can make a difference.

2. **Write a Note**: Consider writing a handwritten note to express your gratitude. A thoughtful note can convey your appreciation in a personal and meaningful way. You can

mention specific acts of kindness or support that meant a lot to you.

3. **Give a Gift**: Small gestures like giving a thoughtful gift can show your appreciation. It doesn't have to be extravagant; even a small token of appreciation can convey your gratitude effectively.

4. **Quality Time**: Spending quality time with someone can be a great way to show appreciation. Whether it's having a meaningful conversation, going for a walk together, or engaging in a shared activity, showing up and being present can speak volumes.

5. **Acts of Service**: Offering to help someone with a task or running an errand for them can show that you appreciate them. Taking action to make someone's life a little easier can be a powerful way to express your gratitude.

6. **Public Acknowledgment**: Sometimes, publicly acknowledging someone's

contributions or kindness can be a meaningful way to show appreciation. This can be done on social media, in front of others, or in a group setting.

7. **Listen and Validate**: Sometimes, all it takes to show appreciation is to actively listen to someone and validate their feelings. Offering a listening ear and being empathetic towards their experiences can go a long way in showing that you appreciate them.

Remember, expressing appreciation is not just about the words you say but also about the sincerity and thoughtfulness behind them. Taking the time to show genuine gratitude can strengthen your relationships and create a positive impact on those around you.

3. Reflect on positive experiences: Regularly reflect on positive experiences and things that bring you joy. Focus on the good things in your life rather than dwelling on the negatives.

Reflecting on positive experiences can have a profound impact on one's well-being and overall outlook on life. By regularly focusing on the good things that have happened, we can cultivate gratitude, resilience, and a more optimistic mindset. It helps us appreciate the simple joys in life and reminds us that there is so much to be thankful for.

Positive reflection can also boost our mood and increase our overall happiness. When we consciously choose to dwell on the positives rather than the negatives, we train our minds to see the silver linings in challenging situations and to savor the moments of joy and contentment.

Taking time each day to reflect on positive experiences can be a powerful tool for self-care and mental well-being. It can provide a sense of perspective and remind us that even in the midst of difficulties, there is always something to be grateful for. So, let's make it a habit to focus on the good, appreciate the positives in our lives, and nurture a mindset of optimism and gratitude.

By regularly reflecting on positive experiences, we create a reservoir of good memories that we can draw upon during tougher times. These memories serve as a source of comfort, reminding us that joy and happiness are not fleeting but can be found in the everyday moments of our lives.

Moreover, focusing on the positives can help shift our perspective and reframe our thinking. It allows us to see challenges as opportunities for growth and learning rather than insurmountable obstacles. This positive mindset can lead to increased motivation, creativity, and a sense of empowerment to tackle whatever comes our way.

In addition, reflecting on positive experiences can strengthen our relationships with others. Sharing moments of joy and gratitude with loved ones can deepen connections and foster a sense of community and belonging. It can also inspire and uplift those around us, creating a ripple effect of positivity and kindness.

Ultimately, regularly reflecting on positive experiences is a simple yet powerful practice that can enhance our overall well-being and enrich our lives. So, let's make a conscious effort to shift our focus towards the good, celebrate the moments of happiness, and cultivate a mindset of positivity and gratitude.

4. Practice mindfulness: Be present in the moment and pay attention to the small details around you. Mindfulness can help you appreciate the beauty in everyday life.

Taking a moment to practice mindfulness can involve focusing on your breathing, tuning in to your senses, and noticing the sights, sounds, and feelings in your immediate surroundings. By being fully present in the moment and immersing yourself in the details of your environment, you can cultivate a sense of gratitude and appreciation for the simple yet beautiful aspects of life that often go unnoticed. Mindfulness can help reduce stress, increase self-awareness, and promote a sense of calm and clarity in your day-to-day experiences. Try incorporating moments of mindfulness into your daily routine to enhance your overall well-being and find joy in the present moment.

Here's a longer response:

Practicing mindfulness involves intentionally directing your attention to the present moment without judgment. It's about being fully engaged in what you're doing, whether it's eating, walking, working, or simply breathing. By tuning into your senses and observing the details around you, you can cultivate a greater awareness of the world and your place in it.

When you practice mindfulness, you give yourself the gift of fully experiencing life as it unfolds, moment by moment. You become more attuned to the beauty of everyday moments that might otherwise pass you by—a gentle breeze, the warmth of sunlight on your skin, the sound of birds chirping, or the taste of your favorite food.

By incorporating mindfulness into your daily routine, you can cultivate a deep sense of gratitude and appreciation for the simple pleasures that surround you. This practice can help you navigate life's ups and downs with greater ease, as you learn to respond to situations from a place of centeredness and clarity.

So, take a few moments each day to practice mindfulness, whether through meditation, deep breathing exercises, or simply pausing to notice the small details around you. Embrace the present moment with an open heart and a curious mind, and let mindfulness led you to a deeper sense of peace and contentment in your daily life.

By nurturing mindfulness, you invite a profound shift in your awareness, enabling you to savor the richness of each passing moment. Through regular practice, you open a gateway to inner peace and resilience, anchoring yourself in the beauty of the present. Embrace stillness, welcome clarity, and let gratitude illuminate your path towards a more harmonious existence. Trust in the power of mindfulness to guide you through life's complexities, offering solace and strength in times of challenge. Be present, breathe deeply, and allow mindfulness to shape a life of serenity and authenticity.

Immerse yourself fully in the tapestry of the present moment, where the symphony of existence unfolds in all its intricate beauty. Let mindfulness be your compass, gently guiding you through the ebbs and flows of life's journey. Embrace each breath as a gift, a portal to inner stillness and profound connection. With each step on this mindful path, you uncover new dimensions of self-awareness and gratitude. Surrender to the magic of the now, where peace resides in the quiet whispers of your soul. Let mindfulness be your loyal companion, leading you towards a life brimming with purpose, joy, and profound wisdom.

5. Count your blessings: Take a moment each day to mentally list things you are grateful for. This practice can shift your focus from what you lack to what you have.

Counting your blessings and practicing gratitude daily can significantly improve your outlook on life, reduce stress, and increase your overall happiness. It shifts your focus from what you lack to what you have, helping you appreciate the little things in life. Gratitude can also improve your relationships, boost your mental health, and increase your resilience in facing life's challenges. So, take a moment each day to acknowledge and be grateful for the good things in your life—it can make a big difference.

Reflecting on the positive aspects of your life not only helps cultivate a sense of gratitude but also fosters a more optimistic mindset. Acknowledging and appreciating the blessings you have can bring a sense of contentment and joy, even during challenging times. By consciously focusing on what you are grateful for, you train your mind to notice and savor the richness of your life. This practice can lead to a more balanced perspective, increased resilience, and a deeper sense of fulfillment. So, take a few moments each day to count your blessings, and watch how it transforms your outlook on life.

Reflecting on the positive aspects of your life can be a powerful way to shift your focus from what may be lacking or challenging towards what is going well. By acknowledging the blessings, you have, whether big or small, you cultivate a sense of appreciation and gratitude that can significantly improve your overall well-being.

Expressing gratitude has been linked to numerous physical and psychological benefits, such as reduced stress, improved relationships, enhanced mood, and even better physical health. When you actively practice gratitude, you train your brain to look for the good in every situation, helping you find silver linings even in difficult moments.

Moreover, fostering a grateful mindset can lead to increased resilience in the face of adversity. By recognizing and appreciating the positives in your life, you develop a more optimistic perspective that can help you navigate challenges with greater ease and confidence.

Taking time each day to reflect on what you are grateful for is a simple yet profound practice that can transform your day-to-day experience. Whether through journaling, meditation, or simply pausing to appreciate the present moment, incorporating gratitude into your daily routine can have a profound impact on your mental and emotional well-being.

So, remember to count your blessings, no matter how small they may seem, and cultivate a sense of gratitude that can enrich your life in ways you may not have imagined.

By focusing on the positive aspects of your life, you create a ripple effect that can extend beyond your own well-being. When you embody gratitude and a sense of contentment, you radiate positivity that can uplift those around you as well. Your gratitude can inspire others to also pause and appreciate the good in their lives, creating a shared sense of joy and connection.

Furthermore, practicing gratitude can help you develop a deeper sense of fulfillment and purpose. By recognizing the blessings in your life, you become more attuned to what truly matters to you and what brings you genuine happiness. This awareness can guide your decisions and actions, leading you towards a more meaningful and fulfilling life.

Additionally, incorporating gratitude into your daily routine can help you cultivate a sense of mindfulness and presence. When you take the time to reflect on what you are grateful for, you anchor yourself in the present moment, fostering a greater sense of awareness and clarity. This mindfulness can enhance your overall mental well-being and help you approach challenges with a more grounded and centered mindset.

In essence, gratitude is a powerful tool that can transform your outlook on life, enhance your relationships, and boost your overall well-being. Remember that gratitude is a practice that grows stronger with consistency and commitment. So, embrace the habit of counting your blessings each day, and open yourself up to a world of positivity, resilience, and fulfillment.

6. Volunteer or help others: Giving back to others can help you appreciate what you have in your life and create feelings of gratitude.

When you volunteer or help others, you not only make a positive impact on someone else's life, but you also gain a sense of fulfillment and purpose. It can help you develop a deeper appreciation for what you have and remind you of the things that truly matter. Additionally, giving back can create feelings of gratitude and satisfaction, ultimately leading to increased happiness and a sense of well-being. So, whether it's through volunteering your time, donating to a cause, or simply helping a friend in need, making a difference in someone else's life can have a powerful and positive effect on your own well-being.

By giving back to others through volunteering and acts of kindness, you not only make a difference in someone else's life but also foster a sense of compassion and gratitude within yourself. This can lead to increased happiness, fulfillment, and a deeper appreciation for the things that truly matter in life. Remember, small gestures of kindness can have a ripple effect, spreading positivity and creating a more connected and caring community.

It's important to realize that even the smallest act of kindness can have a significant impact. Whether it's helping a neighbor, donating to a charity, or simply offering a kind word to someone in need, these actions can create a chain reaction of positivity that can uplift both the giver and the recipient.

Volunteering and spreading kindness not only benefit those directly involved but also contribute to building a more compassionate and supportive society. When individuals come together to support each other, they create a sense of community and belonging that can improve the well-being of all members.

So, next time you have the opportunity to help someone or show kindness, remember that your actions hold the power to make a difference in someone's life and contribute to creating a more empathetic and harmonious world for us all to live in.

By continuing to practice kindness and giving back to others, you can inspire positive change and create a ripple effect of compassion in the world. Remember that every act of kindness, no matter how small, has the potential to make a meaningful impact. So, keep spreading positivity, showing empathy, and lending a helping hand whenever you can. Your actions matter, and they have the power to shape a brighter, more connected future for all.

7. Use positive affirmations: Repeat positive affirmations related to gratitude to help shift your mindset and focus on the positive aspects of your life.

Using positive affirmations involves focusing on statements that promote self-confidence, self-worth, and personal growth. By regularly repeating positive affirmations, you can rewire your subconscious mind to believe in supportive and encouraging thoughts about yourself. This practice can help boost your self-esteem, reduce negative self-talk, and cultivate a more optimistic outlook on life. Examples of positive affirmations include statements like "I am capable and strong," "I deserve love and happiness," and "I embrace challenges as opportunities for growth. "Consistent use of positive affirmations can lead to improved mental well-being and a more positive mindset overall.

Using positive affirmations involves focusing on statements that promote self-confidence, self-worth, and personal growth. By regularly repeating positive affirmations, you can rewire your subconscious mind to believe in supportive and encouraging thoughts about yourself. This practice can help boost your self-esteem, reduce negative self-talk, and cultivate a more optimistic outlook on life.

Examples of positive affirmations include statements like "I am capable and strong," "I deserve love and happiness," and "I embrace challenges as opportunities for growth." Consistent use of positive affirmations can lead to improved mental well-being and a more positive mindset overall.

Incorporating positive affirmations into your daily routine can be a powerful tool for self-improvement and personal development. Whether you say them out loud, write them down, or repeat them silently to yourself, the key is to choose affirmations that resonate with you personally and to practice them regularly. Over time, you may notice a shift in your mindset, increased self-confidence, and a greater sense of self-belief.

Sample

1. I am grateful for all the abundance and blessings in my life.

2. I appreciate the love and support that surrounds me every day.

3. I am thankful for the opportunities that come my way.

4. I choose to see the beauty and joy in every moment.

5. I am grateful for my health and well-being.

6. I am capable of achieving great things, and I am thankful for my potential.

7. I radiate positivity and gratitude, attracting more blessings into my life.

8. I am grateful for the lessons I learn from every experience.

9. I am surrounded by positivity and I am open to receiving all the good that is coming my way.

10. I am grateful for the present moment and all the possibilities it holds.

11. I am filled with gratitude for the kindness and generosity of others.

12. I am thankful for the simple pleasures that bring me joy each day.

13. I am grateful for the growth and personal development that challenges bring into my life.

14. I am blessed with a grateful heart that sees the beauty in every situation.

15. I am grateful for the love I am able to give and receive.

16. I appreciate the beauty of nature and the peace it brings to my soul.

17. I am thankful for the strength and resilience that I possess.

18. I am grateful for the abundance of opportunities that lay before me.

19. I am thankful for the friends and family who
support and uplift me.

20. I am grateful for the gift of life and the
chance to make a positive impact in the world.

"Remember, like any other skill, practicing gratitude takes time and consistency. Over time, you will start to notice a positive shift in your mindset and overall well-being."

11. Engage in activities that bring you joy:

Make time for hobbies and activities that bring you happiness and fulfillment.

Engaging in activities that bring you joy is essential for maintaining a healthy work-life balance and overall well-being. Whether it's painting, dancing, hiking, playing a musical instrument, or practicing yoga, taking time for hobbies and activities that you love can help reduce stress, boost creativity, and improve your mood.

By making time for activities that bring you happiness and fulfillment, you can recharge your energy levels and find a sense of purpose outside of your daily responsibilities. This can also help you build new skills, meet like-minded individuals, and expand your perspective on life.

Remember, self-care isn't selfish—it's necessary for your mental and emotional health. So, prioritize activities that bring you joy and make them a regular part of your routine. Whether it's a few minutes each day or a dedicated block of time each week, investing in your well-being through enjoyable activities is a gift you give yourself.

Exploring different hobbies and activities can also lead to personal growth and self-discovery. When you engage in things that bring you joy, you are giving yourself the opportunity to learn more about your interests, strengths, and preferences. This self-awareness can be valuable in shaping your identity and understanding what brings meaning and fulfillment to your life.

Moreover, participating in hobbies can provide a sense of accomplishment and boost your self-esteem. Seeing progress in a creative project, mastering a new skill, or simply enjoying the process of learning something new can all contribute to a greater sense of confidence and satisfaction.

In today's fast-paced world, it can be easy to overlook the importance of leisure and recreation. However, setting aside time for activities that bring you joy is not indulgent—it is a fundamental aspect of self-care and overall well-being. So, whether it's reading a book, gardening, cooking, or practicing meditation, find what resonates with you and make it a priority in your life. You deserve to experience moments of joy and fulfillment amidst your daily responsibilities.

Engaging in activities that bring you joy is essential for your mental and emotional well-being. Here are some steps you can take to incorporate joy into your life:

1. Identify what brings you joy: Take some time to reflect on activities, hobbies, or experiences that make you feel happy and fulfilled.

2. Make time for joy: Schedule regular time in your day or week to engage in activities that bring you joy. Prioritize these activities just as you would any other obligation.

3. Try new things: Be open to trying new activities or hobbies that you haven't explored before. You might discover new sources of joy.

4. Practice mindfulness: Be present in the moment and fully engage in the activity you're doing. This can help you appreciate the joy it brings.

5. Surround yourself with positivity: Spend time with people who uplift you and create a positive environment that nurtures your joy.

6. Spread joy to others: Share your joy with others by engaging in activities together or by simply spreading positivity and kindness.

7. Set realistic expectations: Don't put too much pressure on yourself to achieve a certain level

of perfection in your activities. Focus on enjoying the process rather than the outcome.

8. Create a joy list: Make a list of activities or experiences that bring you joy and refer to it when you're looking for inspiration on how to lift your mood.

9. Engage in self-care: Taking care of your physical and mental well-being through practices like exercise, meditation, or spending time in nature can help boost your overall sense of joy.

10. Gratitude practice: Cultivate a practice of gratitude by reflecting on the things in your life that bring you joy and expressing thanks for them.

11. Mix it up: Keep things interesting by varying the activities you engage in to prevent boredom and maintain your sense of excitement and joy.

12. Reflect and adjust: Pay attention to how different activities make you feel and make adjustments based on what brings you the most joy and fulfillment.

"Remember, joy is a personal and individual experience, so it's important to explore what works best for you and incorporate those activities into your routine regularly. Prioritizing joy can have a significant impact on your overall happiness and well-being."

12. Develop a self-care routine:

Create a routine that includes activities like exercise, proper nutrition, quality sleep, and relaxation techniques to take care of your physical and mental well-being.

Developing a self-care routine means establishing a set of practices or activities that help you prioritize your physical, mental, and emotional well-being. This routine typically involves activities that promote relaxation, stress relief, and overall health. Self-care routines can include things like meditation, exercise, healthy eating, skincare, journaling, spending time in nature, and engaging in hobbies that bring you joy. By incorporating these practices into your daily or weekly routine, you can better manage stress, improve your mental health, and enhance your overall well-being.

Developing a self-care routine involves identifying your specific needs and preferences, experimenting with different activities to find what works best for you, and making a commitment to consistently engage in these practices. It's important to be proactive about taking care of yourself and to prioritize self-care as an essential part of your daily life. Remember that self-care is not selfish—it is necessary for maintaining your physical, mental, and emotional health. By creating a self-care routine that works for you, you can boost your overall well-being and better cope with the challenges of everyday life.

Here's a sample self-care routine that incorporates various activities to take care of your physical and mental well-being:

**Morning Routine: **
1. **Wake Up Early: ** Start your day with a peaceful morning routine to avoid feeling rushed.

2. **Exercise: ** Engage in a 20–30-minute workout session. This can be yoga, a brisk walk, or a home workout routine.

3. **Healthy Breakfast: ** Fuel your body with a nutritious breakfast - include fruits, whole grains, and protein.

4. **Mindfulness Practice: ** Spend a few minutes meditating or practicing deep breathing exercises to center yourself for the day ahead.

**Daytime Routine: **
1. **Stay Hydrated: ** Drink plenty of water throughout the day to stay hydrated.

2. **Healthy Snacks: ** opt for healthy snacks like nuts, fruits, or yogurt to keep your energy levels up.

3. **Lunch Break: ** Take a break from work to enjoy a balanced lunch with vegetables, lean protein, and whole grains.

4. **Stretch Breaks: ** Take short breaks every hour to stretch your body and prevent stiffness from prolonged sitting.

**Evening Routine: **
1. **Healthy Dinner: ** Prepare a balanced dinner with lean protein, vegetables, and complex carbs.

2. **Digital Detox: ** Limit screen time before bed to ensure quality sleep. Engage in relaxing activities like reading a book or taking a bath.

3. **Bedtime Routine: ** Wind down with a calming bedtime routine - practice gentle yoga, listen to soothing music, or write in a journal.

4. **Quality Sleep: ** Aim for 7-8 hours of quality sleep each night to allow your body and mind to rest and rejuvenate.

**Weekly Self-Care Practices: **
1. **Outdoor Activities: ** Spend time outdoors in nature to recharge and rejuvenate.

2. **Social Connection: ** Connect with friends or family members to maintain social connections and support systems.

3. **Hobbies: ** Engage in activities you enjoy, whether it's painting, gardening, or playing a musical instrument.

4. **Self-Reflection: ** Take time for self-reflection through journaling or mindfulness practices to check in with your emotions and thoughts.

Remember, self-care is personal, so feel free to customize this routine to suit your preferences and lifestyle. Prioritize activities that make you feel good and support your overall well-being.

Self-care can take many forms, such as physical activities like exercise, yoga, or going for a walk, as well as mental and emotional activities like journaling, meditation, or spending time with loved ones. Remember to listen to your body and mind to determine what you need in the moment. Engaging in self-care practices regularly can help reduce stress, improve your mood, and enhance your overall well-being. It's essential to carve out time for yourself amidst the demands of daily life and make self-care a priority. So, take a moment to reflect on what activities bring you joy and relaxation, and incorporate them into your daily routine. Remember, you deserve to prioritize your own well-being and happiness.

Self-care is a personal journey that involves identifying your needs, setting boundaries, and making choices that prioritize your well-being. It's about taking intentional actions to nurture your physical, emotional, and mental health. Self-care looks different for everyone, so it's important to explore activities that resonate with you and make you feel good.

Physical self-care can include activities like exercising, eating well, getting enough sleep, and engaging in relaxing activities like taking a bath or getting a massage. Mental and emotional self-care involve practices such as mindfulness, meditation, journaling, therapy, or engaging in hobbies that bring you joy.

Self-care isn't just about indulgence or pampering; it's about building resilience, managing stress, and fostering a positive relationship with yourself. It's about recognizing when you need a break or extra support and giving yourself permission to prioritize your well-being.

"Remember that self-care is a continuous practice, and it's okay to adjust your self-care routine as needed based on your current circumstances and emotions. By making self-care a priority in your life, you are investing in your long-term health and happiness."

13. Stay true to yourself:

Embrace your uniqueness and authenticity, and don't be afraid to stand up for what you believe in.

"Stay true to yourself" means to be authentic, genuine, and honest with who you are as a person. It involves staying loyal to your values, beliefs, and principles, even when faced with challenges or pressure to conform to others' expectations.

Staying true to yourself means being genuine and authentic in your thoughts, actions, and interactions with others. It involves aligning your behavior with your values, beliefs, and principles, even when faced with external pressures or expectations. By staying true to yourself, you are more likely to live a fulfilling and meaningful life that reflects your true identity and essence.

It's important to stay true to yourself and embrace your uniqueness. Stand up for what you believe in, even if it means going against the crowd. Authenticity is empowering and attracts like-minded individuals who appreciate the real you. Celebrate your individuality and trust your instincts. By staying true to yourself, you not only honor your values but also inspire others to do the same. Embrace your authenticity, be proud of who you are, and let your light shine bright in the world.

Embrace your uniqueness and authenticity, and stand up for what you believe in. By being true to yourself, you inspire others to do the same. Stay authentic, be proud of who you are, and let your light shine brightly.

Staying true to yourself involves being authentic and honest with yourself about your values, beliefs, and goals. Here are some tips to help you stay true to yourself:

1. **Know Yourself: ** Take the time to understand your values, beliefs, and strengths. Reflect on what is important to you and what you stand for.

Knowing yourself is a journey of self-discovery that involves introspection, reflection, and self-awareness. By taking the time to understand your values, beliefs, and strengths, you can gain clarity on who you are as an individual and what matters most to you. Reflecting on what is important to you can help you make decisions aligned with your authentic self and live a more fulfilling life.

Understanding your values involves identifying the principles and ideals that guide your choices and actions. These can include things like honesty, integrity, compassion, or creativity. By knowing your values, you can make decisions that are in alignment with what matters most to you.

Understanding your beliefs involves examining your thoughts, attitudes, and perspectives on various aspects of life. Your beliefs shape your mindset and influence how you perceive the world around you. By becoming aware of your beliefs, you can challenge any limiting or negative beliefs that may be holding you back and cultivate more empowering beliefs that support your growth and well-being.

Understanding your strengths involves recognizing your unique talents, skills, and abilities. By focusing on your strengths, you can leverage them to achieve your goals, overcome challenges, and thrive in your endeavors. Knowing your strengths can also help you build confidence and self-esteem as you acknowledge and appreciate your capabilities.

Reflecting on your values, beliefs, and strengths can provide valuable insights into who you are as a person and how you want to show up in the world. It can help you make decisions that are true to yourself, set meaningful goals that align with your values, and live a more purposeful and authentic life. Remember that self-discovery is an ongoing process, so continue to explore and learn more about yourself as you grow and evolve.

Understanding your values, beliefs, and strengths is essential for personal growth and self-improvement. When you have a deep awareness of what truly matters to you, what you stand for, and what you excel at, you can make better choices that lead to a more meaningful and fulfilling life. Reflect on your experiences, listen to your inner voice, and pay attention to how you respond to different situations. By knowing yourself well, you can build confidence, resilience, and a strong sense of self-identity. Embrace the process of self-discovery as an opportunity for growth and transformation, and embrace all aspects of who you are, both your strengths and areas for development.

2. **Set Boundaries: ** Learn to say no to things that don't align with your values or make you uncomfortable. Setting boundaries is essential for staying true to yourself.

Setting boundaries can help protect your mental and emotional well-being. It's okay to prioritize your needs and make choices that serve your best interests. Remember, saying no is not selfish; it's a way of taking care of yourself and maintaining your authenticity. By setting boundaries, you define what is acceptable and unacceptable in your interactions with others, leading to healthier relationships and greater self-respect. Remember that you have the right to advocate for yourself and your well-being.

Setting boundaries also involves communicating your limits clearly and assertively to others. It's important to express your needs and expectations in a calm and respectful manner. Be firm in enforcing your boundaries and don't feel guilty for prioritizing your own well-being. Remember that boundaries are not meant to push people away, but rather to establish mutual respect and understanding in relationships.

Additionally, recognizing when your boundaries are being crossed is crucial. Pay attention to your feelings and emotions, as they can serve as indicators that a boundary violation has occurred. Trust your instincts and take action to address the situation if needed.

Lastly, be consistent in upholding your boundaries. Practice self-care and self-compassion to maintain your boundaries effectively. Surround yourself with supportive individuals who respect and appreciate your boundaries. Remember, setting boundaries is a powerful act of self-care and self-respect, and it is essential for living authentically and in alignment with your values.

3. **Listen to Your Inner Voice: ** Trust your instincts and listen to your intuition. Your inner

voice can guide you in making decisions that feel right for you.

"Listen to your inner voice" generally means paying attention to your intuition, instincts, and inner feelings in order to make decisions and choices that are more aligned with your true self. It encourages you to trust your own thoughts and feelings rather than solely relying on external influences or opinions. By listening to your inner voice, you can often find guidance, clarity, and authenticity in your actions and decisions.

Listening to your inner voice involves reflecting on your thoughts, feelings, and desires without the interference of external distractions. It requires tuning in to your intuition and recognizing the signals and messages that come from within. This practice can help you make decisions that feel right for you, rather than being swayed by societal expectations or the opinions of others.

Your inner voice is often a source of wisdom and guidance, speaking to you in moments of uncertainty or confusion. By paying attention to this inner guidance, you can navigate life's challenges with more clarity and authenticity. Trusting your inner voice can lead to a deeper sense of self-awareness and personal growth as you learn to honor your own values, needs, and aspirations.

In a world filled with noise and distractions, taking the time to listen to your inner voice can offer a sense of grounding and alignment with your true self. It is a practice that allows you to connect with your intuition and cultivate a greater sense of self-trust. By embracing and honoring your inner voice, you can live a more authentic, purposeful, and fulfilling life.

Your inner voice is like a compass that points you in the right direction. Take the time to tune into it, reflect on your thoughts and feelings, and trust the wisdom that comes from within. When you listen to your inner voice, you can navigate through life with more clarity, confidence, and authenticity. So, trust yourself and let your inner voice be your guiding light. Trust that the whispers of your inner voice hold valuable insights and truths that can lead you towards your path of purpose and fulfillment. By quieting the external noise and distractions, you can better hear the gentle nudges and guidance that your intuition provides. Embrace the power of your intuition as a valuable tool in navigating life's challenges and opportunities. Remember, your inner voice is there to support and empower you as you journey through life's twists and turns. So, trust, listen, and follow its guidance with open-heartedness and courage.

4. **Surround Yourself with Supportive People: ** Surround yourself with people who accept and support you for who you are. Avoid individuals who try to change you or undermine your authenticity.

Having a strong support system can help you feel more confident, empowered, and capable of achieving your goals. Surrounding yourself with supportive people who celebrate your successes and offer encouragement during challenging times can make a significant difference in your overall well-being. It's essential to cultivate relationships with individuals who appreciate you for your true self and provide a positive influence in your life.

By prioritizing relationships with supportive individuals, you create a nurturing environment that fosters personal growth and emotional stability. These supportive connections can offer valuable perspectives, advice, and empathy when you need it most. Moreover, being surrounded by people who believe in you can inspire you to pursue your passions and overcome obstacles with confidence.

In contrast, toxic relationships can drain your energy, diminish your self-esteem, and impede your personal development. It's important to recognize when certain individuals are not contributing positively to your life and take steps to distance yourself from their influence. Remember that you deserve to be surrounded by people who uplift and encourage you, rather than bring you down.

Ultimately, building a network of supportive relationships is a key component of maintaining a healthy and fulfilling life. Seek out those who bring out the best in you and foster an environment where you can thrive both personally and professionally. Remember, you have the power to choose who you surround yourself with, so choose wisely and prioritize those who genuinely care about your well-being and success.

Surrounding yourself with supportive people not only benefits your mental and emotional well-being but also contributes to your overall sense of fulfillment and happiness. The positive energy and encouragement you receive from a strong support system can help you navigate life's challenges with resilience and optimism. Remember to invest in relationships that nurture your growth and well-being, and don't hesitate to let go of toxic influences that hinder your progress. Prioritize genuine connections that align with your values and aspirations, and cultivate a community that uplifts and empowers you to be the best version of yourself.

5. **Practice Self-Care: ** Take care of your physical, mental, and emotional well-being. Self-care helps you stay grounded and connected with yourself.

Self-care can include activities such as exercising, meditating, getting enough sleep, spending time with loved ones, practicing gratitude, and engaging in hobbies or activities that bring you joy and relaxation. Taking care of yourself is essential for maintaining overall well-being and reducing stress.

Here are some additional self-care practices you can consider incorporating into your routine:

1. Practice mindfulness or deep breathing exercises to help calm your mind and reduce stress.

2. Engage in activities that promote relaxation, such as taking a warm bath, reading a book, or listening to calming music.

3. Prioritize self-care by setting boundaries and saying no to things that drain your energy.

4. Stay hydrated, eat nourishing foods, and get regular exercise to support your physical health.

5. Connect with nature by spending time outdoors or bringing natural elements into your home.

6. Talk to a friend or therapist about your feelings and emotions to process and release any pent-up stress or tension.

7. Schedule time for activities that recharge you, whether it's a solo walk-in nature or a fun outing with friends.

Remember, self-care is a personal practice, so it's important to explore and find what works best for you.

6. **Stay Open-Minded and Growth-oriented: ** While staying true to yourself is crucial, it's also essential to remain open-minded and willing to learn and grow. Embrace new experiences and perspectives that enrich your life.

"Stay open-minded and growth-oriented" means being receptive to new ideas, perspectives, and experiences, while also being focused on personal development and improvement. It involves being willing to learn, adapt, and grow in various aspects of life.

By staying open-minded and growth-oriented, you can expand your horizons, develop new skills, and foster personal development.

Embracing different perspectives and experiences can lead to increased empathy, creativity, and resilience, ultimately enhancing your overall well-being and success in various aspects of life.

Continuing to approach life with an open mind can lead to discovering new opportunities, building deeper relationships, and becoming more adaptable in the face of challenges. Remember that growth often comes from stepping out of your comfort zone and being receptive to diverse viewpoints and ideas.

Approaching life with an open mind allows for personal growth, new opportunities, deeper relationships, and increased adaptability in the face of challenges. Embracing diverse viewpoints and ideas can lead to valuable insights and enriching experiences.

When you approach life with an open mind, you invite the world to unfold before you in unexpected and beautiful ways. By being receptive to diverse viewpoints and ideas, you expand your horizons and enrich your understanding of the world around you. This openness can lead to newfound passions, insights, and connections that can transform your life in profound ways.

Stepping out of your comfort zone is often where growth truly happens. It is in those moments of discomfort and uncertainty that you discover your true capabilities and potential. Embracing challenges with an open mind allows you to learn, adapt, and evolve, making you more resilient and resourceful in the face of adversity.

Moreover, building deeper relationships is another significant benefit of approaching life with an open mind. When you are receptive to others' perspectives and ideas, you foster understanding, empathy, and connection. This deepens your relationships with others, creating a network of support and companionship that can sustain you through life's ups and downs.

Ultimately, embracing an open mind is a powerful tool for personal growth and fulfillment. It allows you to navigate life with curiosity, courage, and resilience, opening yourself up to a world of possibilities and potential. So, remember to keep your mind open, your heart receptive, and your spirit adventurous as you journey through life's endless opportunities and challenges.

7. **Express Yourself: ** Communicate your thoughts, feelings, and ideas authentically. Express yourself creatively through art, writing, music, or any other outlet that resonates with you.

Expressing yourself is a beautiful and powerful way to connect with others and with yourself. It's important to share your thoughts, feelings, and ideas authentically, whether through art, writing, music, or any other form of expression that speaks to you. Creativity allows you to tap into your true self and communicate in ways that words alone sometimes can't. So, don't be afraid to explore different outlets and express yourself freely. Your unique voice and perspective are valuable and deserve to be shared with the world.

Absolutely - expressing yourself is not just about sharing your thoughts, feelings, and ideas, but also about discovering more about yourself in the process. When you engage in creative outlets like art, writing, music, or any other form of expression, you delve into the depths of your emotions and experiences. This exploration can lead to new insights, self-discovery, and personal growth. By expressing yourself authentically, you not only share a piece of who you are with others but also deepen your connection to your own innermost thoughts and feelings. It's a journey of self-discovery and connection that can be truly transformative.

Expressing yourself can take many forms, and it's different for everyone. Here are some ways you can express yourself:

1. **Art: ** Create art, whether it's painting, drawing, sculpting, or any other form of artistic expression.

2. **Writing: ** Keep a journal, write poetry, or start a blog. Writing can be a powerful way to express your thoughts and emotions.

3. **Music: ** Play an instrument, write songs, or simply listen to music that resonates with you.

4. **Dance: ** Use movement to express yourself and your emotions. Dance can be a powerful form of self-expression.

5. **Talking: ** Have open and honest conversations with trusted friends or family members about how you're feeling.

6. **Fashion: ** Experiment with different clothing styles that make you feel confident and reflect your personality.

7. **Photography: ** Capture moments and scenes that inspire you or convey a certain emotion.

8. **Cooking: ** Express your creativity through cooking and trying out new recipes.

9. **Physical activity: ** Exercise, yoga, or sports can help release pent-up emotions and express yourself physically.

10. **Mindfulness practices: ** Engage in activities like meditation, deep breathing, or mindfulness to connect with yourself and understand your emotions better.

Remember, expressing yourself is a personal journey, so explore different avenues until you find what feels most authentic and fulfilling to you.

8. **Trust Yourself: ** Believe in your abilities and trust your decisions. Self-confidence is key to staying true to yourself in the face of challenges or criticism.

Believe in your inner voice and intuition. Trust that you have the strength and capability to overcome obstacles and achieve your goals. Remember that you are deserving of success and happiness, and trust that you have what it takes to make your dreams a reality. When you trust yourself, you exude a sense of confidence that can inspire others and help you navigate through life's ups and downs with grace and resilience. Trusting yourself is the first step towards creating a life that is authentic and fulfilling.

Believing in yourself is an ongoing journey that requires practice and self-reflection. Take the time to celebrate your successes, no matter how small they may seem, and learn from your failures to grow stronger and more resilient. Surround yourself with supportive and uplifting people who believe in you and your capabilities. Remember that self-doubt is natural, but it's important not to let it hold you back from pursuing your passions and aspirations.

Trust in your intuition and listen to your inner voice when making decisions. Pay attention to your instincts and feelings, as they can guide you towards the path that is right for you. As you trust yourself more, you'll find it easier to set boundaries, make choices that align with your values, and stay true to who you are.

Developing self-trust takes time and effort, but it is a crucial ingredient for living a fulfilling and authentic life. Embrace your uniqueness, cultivate your strengths, and have faith in your ability to overcome challenges and obstacles. By trusting yourself, you empower yourself to create the life you truly desire and deserve. Trust in yourself, and the possibilities are endless.

"Remember, staying true to yourself is a journey that requires self-awareness, self-acceptance, and self-respect. It's about being comfortable in your own skin and living authentically in a way that feels right for you."

14. Keep learning and growing:

Stay curious and open-minded, and continue to seek opportunities for personal and professional growth.

Learning and growing are processes that never end. Keep pushing yourself to acquire new knowledge, develop new skills, and expand your capabilities. Embrace challenges, stay curious, and remain open to new experiences. This mindset of continuous learning and growth will not only enrich your life but also lead to personal and professional success.

Keep learning and growing is a mindset that encourages you to continuously seek knowledge and self-improvement. It involves being open to new ideas, perspectives, and experiences that can help you expand your horizons and develop as a person. By constantly challenging yourself, stepping out of your comfort zone, and embracing change, you can unlock your full potential and achieve personal and professional growth. Remember, growth is a journey, not a destination, so stay committed to learning, evolving, and becoming the best version of yourself.

Embracing a mindset of continuous learning and growth can lead to numerous benefits in various aspects of your life. Here are some key advantages:

1. **Personal Development**: Constantly seeking new knowledge and experiences can help you discover more about yourself, your values, and your passions. This self-awareness is crucial for personal growth and can lead to increased confidence and a stronger sense of purpose.

By actively engaging in personal development through learning new skills, trying new activities, and reflecting on your experiences, you can enhance your self-awareness and gain a deeper understanding of who you are and what drives you. This process of self-discovery can help you identify your strengths and weaknesses, clarify your values and beliefs, and uncover your true passions and interests.

As you become more self-aware, you can set meaningful goals that align with your values and aspirations, leading to a greater sense of direction and purpose in life. Personal growth often involves stepping out of your comfort zone, taking risks, and challenging yourself to overcome obstacles. Through this process, you can build resilience, develop new capabilities, and expand your perspective on the world.

Increasing your self-awareness and personal development can also boost your confidence and self-esteem. When you have a better understanding of yourself and your abilities, you are more likely to believe in your potential and pursue your goals with determination. This confidence can help you overcome self-doubt and fear of failure, allowing you to take on new challenges and thrive in various aspects of your life.

In conclusion, personal development is a continuous journey of self-discovery and growth that can empower you to live a more fulfilling and meaningful life. By seeking new knowledge and experiences, reflecting on your values and passions, and setting goals that align with your true self, you can enhance your self-awareness, boost your confidence, and find a deeper sense of purpose and fulfillment.

To further support your personal development journey, it can be helpful to engage in regular self-reflection and introspection. Take the time to assess your current skills, interests, and values, and consider how they align with your long-term goals and aspirations. Reflect on your past experiences, both successes, and failures, and extract valuable lessons that can guide your future decisions and actions.

Seeking feedback from trusted friends, mentors, or coaches can also provide valuable insights into your strengths and areas for improvement. Be open to constructive criticism and use it as an opportunity for growth and self-improvement. Remember that personal development is a continuous process, and it's okay to make mistakes along the way. Embrace challenges and setbacks as learning opportunities that can help you grow and evolve as a person.

In addition to self-reflection and feedback, consider setting specific, achievable goals for your personal growth. Break down your goals into smaller, manageable steps and create a plan to work towards them systematically. Celebrate your progress and accomplishments along the way, no matter how small, as this will help you stay motivated and committed to your personal development journey.

Furthermore, prioritize self-care and well-being as essential components of personal development. Take care of your physical, emotional, and mental health by incorporating healthy habits such as exercise, proper nutrition, mindfulness practices, and adequate rest. Building a strong foundation of well-being will provide you with the energy and resilience needed to face challenges and pursue your personal growth goals with vigor and determination.

Ultimately, personal development is a transformative process that can lead to greater self-awareness, confidence, and fulfillment. By actively engaging in self-discovery, learning, and growth, you can unlock your full potential, achieve your goals, and live a more purposeful and meaningful life. Embrace the journey of personal development with curiosity, commitment, and openness, and watch yourself evolve into the best version of yourself.

2. **Professional Growth**: In the fast-changing world we live in, those who are committed to learning and adapting tend to excel in their

careers. Continuous learning can provide you with new skills, insights, and perspectives that are valuable in the workplace and can lead to career advancement.

Continuous learning can take many forms, such as attending workshops, taking online courses, reading books, participating in webinars, seeking mentorship, or engaging in hands-on projects. By consistently seeking out new knowledge and experiences, you can stay ahead of the curve in your field, broaden your expertise, and demonstrate your commitment to personal and professional growth.

Moreover, embracing a growth mindset, where you see challenges as opportunities for learning and development, can help you navigate obstacles and setbacks with resilience and determination. By cultivating a mindset that values learning and improvement, you can build confidence in your abilities and adapt to the evolving demands of the workplace.

Ultimately, investing in your continuous learning not only benefits your individual career growth but also brings value to your organization. By staying informed about emerging trends, technologies, and best practices, you can contribute fresh ideas, innovative solutions, and a competitive edge to your team and company.

In summary, embracing continuous learning as a core part of your professional development can open up new opportunities, enhance your skill set, and empower you to thrive in a rapidly changing work environment. By committing to ongoing learning and adaptation, you can position yourself for long-term success and fulfillment in your career.

By actively seeking out opportunities for growth and development, you can build a solid foundation for your career progression, increase your job satisfaction, and establish yourself as a valuable asset in your industry. Remember that learning is a lifelong journey, and the more you invest in your continuous development, the more equipped you'll be to navigate the challenges and changes that come your way. Stay curious, stay engaged, and embrace the power of continuous learning to unlock your full potential and achieve your professional goals.

3. **Resilience**: By being open to challenges and change, you develop resilience and the ability to adapt to new situations. This flexibility can help you navigate obstacles and setbacks more effectively, ultimately leading to greater success and satisfaction.

Resilience is the ability to adapt and bounce back in the face of adversity, challenges, or trauma. It involves coping with stress and difficult situations while maintaining a positive outlook and finding ways to overcome obstacles.

Resilience encompasses a range of skills and traits, including the ability to regulate emotions, develop problem-solving skills, cultivate social connections, and maintain a sense of optimism and hope. It is not just about enduring tough times but also about learning and growing from them. Resilient individuals are better equipped to navigate life's ups and downs and to emerge stronger and more capable as a result. Building resilience often involves developing self-awareness, practicing mindfulness, seeking support from others, and finding healthy ways to cope with stress. It is a valuable quality that can help individuals thrive in the face of challenges and setbacks.

By being open to challenges and change, you develop resilience and the ability to adapt to new situations. This flexibility can help you navigate obstacles and setbacks more effectively, ultimately leading to greater success and satisfaction.

4. **Creativity and Innovation**: Learning and growth stimulate creativity by exposing you to different perspectives and ideas. This can fuel

innovation in your work and personal projects, allowing you to approach problems in novel ways and come up with unique solutions.

Creativity involves the ability to think outside the box, challenge the status quo, and generate new and original ideas. By constantly seeking out new experiences, learning from diverse sources, and staying open-minded, you are more likely to nurture your creativity. This can be through reading books, attending workshops, traveling to different places, engaging in hobbies, or even having deep conversations with people from various backgrounds.

When you expose yourself to a wide range of influences, you broaden your perspective and connect seemingly unrelated dots. This can lead to innovative breakthroughs in your work, whether it's coming up with a new product feature, finding a more efficient process, or designing a creative marketing campaign.

Moreover, creativity and innovation often go hand in hand. While creativity involves generating ideas, innovation is about implementing those ideas to create value. By combining your creative thinking with a drive for action and problem-solving, you can turn your novel ideas into tangible outcomes that make a difference in your projects or endeavors.

In conclusion, never underestimate the power of constantly learning and growing in fueling your creativity and fostering innovation. Embrace new challenges, seek diverse perspectives, and push yourself outside your comfort zone to unlock your full creative potential and drive meaningful innovation.

By immersing yourself in a learning mindset and actively seeking out opportunities for growth, you not only expand your knowledge base but also cultivate the skills necessary to push boundaries and disrupt the norm. Innovation thrives in environments where creativity is nurtured, where diverse ideas are welcomed, and where collaboration is encouraged.

One way to foster creativity and innovation is to create a space that supports experimentation and risk-taking. Encourage yourself to explore unconventional approaches, embrace failure as a learning opportunity, and iterate on your ideas to refine them further. By being open to feedback and willing to adapt, you can iterate on your initial concepts and refine them into truly innovative solutions.

Collaboration with others is also crucial in the creative and innovative process. By engaging with a diverse group of individuals who bring different perspectives and expertise to the table, you can leverage collective creativity to generate more robust and impactful solutions. Through effective communication, active listening, and mutual respect, you can harness the power of teamwork to drive innovation forward.

Ultimately, the journey towards fostering creativity and innovation is a continuous one. It requires dedication, persistence, and a willingness to embrace change and uncertainty. By committing to lifelong learning, staying curious, and remaining open to new possibilities, you can position yourself for success in unleashing your creative potential and driving innovation in all aspects of your life.

5. **Connecting with Others**: A mindset of continuous learning can also help you build stronger relationships with others. By being open to new ideas and experiences, you can engage more deeply with people from diverse backgrounds and perspectives, leading to richer connections and collaborations.

When you approach interactions with a mindset of continuous learning, you demonstrate curiosity and a willingness to listen and understand. This attitude can foster empathy and reduce judgment, allowing you to appreciate the unique experiences and viewpoints of others. As a result, your relationships can become more meaningful and authentic, based on mutual respect and understanding.

Moreover, by actively seeking out new knowledge and skills, you can bring fresh insights and perspectives to your interactions with others. This can lead to stimulating conversations, creative problem-solving, and innovative collaborations, as you combine your diverse areas of expertise with those of your peers.

Overall, cultivating a mindset of continuous learning can not only enrich your own personal growth but also enhance your relationships with others, creating a supportive and inclusive environment where everyone can thrive and contribute their best.

In addition, a mindset of continuous learning can help you navigate differences and conflicts more effectively in your relationships. By approaching challenging situations with a growth-oriented mindset, you can see them as opportunities for understanding, growth, and resolution, rather than obstacles or threats. This mindset can enable you to communicate more openly and constructively, seek common ground, and find creative solutions that benefit all parties involved.

Furthermore, when you engage in lifelong learning, you demonstrate a willingness to adapt and evolve, which can make you more flexible and resilient in your relationships. Instead of being stuck in old patterns or ways of thinking, you are willing to embrace change and new possibilities, which can inspire and motivate those around you to do the same.

Overall, a mindset of continuous learning can transform your relationships with others into dynamic and enriching experiences, where you can learn, grow, and thrive together. By fostering a culture of curiosity, empathy, and collaboration, you can create strong and lasting connections with people from all walks of life, leading to a more fulfilling and rewarding interpersonal journey.

6. **Happiness and Fulfillment**: Engaging in lifelong learning and personal growth can bring a sense of fulfillment and meaning to your life. The process of challenging yourself, setting goals, and achieving them can lead to a greater sense of happiness and satisfaction.

By embracing lifelong learning and personal growth, you are opening yourself up to new experiences, perspectives, and skills. This continuous process can help you break out of your comfort zone, expand your horizons, and discover new passions and interests. As you learn and grow, you may also develop a deeper sense of self-awareness and understanding of your values and purpose in life, which can contribute to a greater overall sense of fulfillment and happiness. Additionally, the sense of accomplishment that comes from setting and achieving goals, no matter how big or small, can boost your confidence and self-esteem, leading to increased levels of satisfaction and well-being.

To find happiness and fulfillment, consider the following tips:

1. **Practice Gratitude: ** Take time every day to focus on the things you are grateful for. This can help shift your perspective to a more positive outlook on life.

2. **Engage in Activities you Enjoy: ** Make time for activities that bring you joy and satisfaction, whether it's a hobby, spending time with loved ones, or pursuing personal goals.

3. **Cultivate Positive Relationships: ** Surround yourself with supportive and positive people who lift you up and make you feel valued. Building strong connections with others can greatly contribute to your sense of fulfillment.

4. **Take Care of Your Physical and Mental Health: ** Make self-care a priority by getting enough sleep, eating well, exercising regularly, and managing stress effectively. Your overall well-being directly impacts your happiness levels.

5. **Set Meaningful Goals: ** Define what is important to you and set goals that align with your values and aspirations. Working towards objectives that are personally meaningful can give you a sense of purpose and fulfillment.

6. **Practice Mindfulness: ** Being present in the moment and practicing mindfulness can help you appreciate life more fully and reduce stress and anxiety.

7. **Contribute to Others: ** Engaging in acts of kindness and helping others can boost your sense of fulfillment and happiness. Making a positive impact on someone else's life can be incredibly rewarding.

8. **Celebrate Small Wins: ** Acknowledge and celebrate your achievements, no matter how small. Recognizing your progress and accomplishments can boost your self-esteem and overall happiness.

9. **Practice Self-compassion: ** Treat yourself with kindness and understanding, especially during times of struggle or difficulty. Practice self-compassion by speaking to yourself as you would to a friend in need.

10. **Engage in Mindful Activities: ** Find activities that bring you into the present moment, such as meditation, yoga, or simply taking a nature walk. Being mindful can help reduce stress and increase feelings of happiness.

11. **Learn and Grow: ** Keep challenging yourself to learn new things and grow as a person. Personal development and continuous learning can lead to a deeper sense of fulfillment.

12. **Spend Time in Nature: ** Connecting with nature has been shown to improve mood and overall well-being. Take time to appreciate the beauty of the natural world and immerse yourself in outdoor activities.

13. **Practice Forgiveness: ** Let go of grudges and practice forgiveness, both towards yourself and others. Holding onto negative emotions can hinder your ability to experience true happiness.

14. **Express Gratitude to Others: ** Show your appreciation for the people in your life by expressing gratitude. Thanking others for their support and kindness can strengthen your relationships and foster a sense of connection.

15. **Create a Balanced Life: ** Strive for balance in all areas of your life, including work, relationships, hobbies, and self-care. Balancing your responsibilities and interests can lead to a more fulfilling and satisfying life.

Remember, happiness is a journey, and it's okay to have ups and downs along the way. By incorporating these tips into your daily life and staying true to yourself, you can cultivate a greater sense of happiness and fulfillment.

Epilogue.

Perspective from the author of the book. Many books were written to give encouragement. or any inspiration or content similar to this book It is the reading that has been given. Thoughts from the point of view Group of people with social, economic, family and income disparities. Success in life of each person will have different foundations and costs of life. As a result, success in the matters we do is not equal or takes the same amount of time. Some people take longer than those with basic background or capital. Life is better. Some people already have good life capital. You will evolve and develop a good quality of life to the next level.

Therefore, do not randomly compare your own qualities with others. There will be more suffering than happiness.

Life is a journey filled with twists and turns, highs and lows, successes and failures. Each individual's path is unique, shaped by their circumstances, choices, and experiences. It's important to remember that success is not a one-size-fits-all concept. What may come easily to one person may require immense effort and sacrifice from another.

In a world where disparities in social status, economic opportunities, family support, and income prevail, it's crucial to recognize that not everyone starts off on an equal footing. Some individuals may have access to resources, privileges, and opportunities that others can only dream of. Yet, this doesn't diminish the value of one's own journey or accomplishments.

Life is a marathon, not a sprint. Some may reach their goals swiftly, while others may face obstacles and setbacks along the way. It's essential to stay focused on your own journey, rather than comparing yourself to others. Remember, comparisons often lead to unnecessary suffering and discontent.

Regardless of where you come from or what challenges you may face, the key lies in perseverance, resilience, and a commitment to personal growth. Embrace your unique path, celebrate your victories - no matter how small - and learn from your struggles. Success is not just about reaching a destination; it's about the growth, learning, and transformation that occur along the way.

So, as you navigate life's uncertainties and complexities, remember that your journey is your own, and it's filled with infinite possibilities for growth and fulfillment. Cherish your experiences, learn from them, and trust in your ability to overcome whatever challenges come your way. In the end, it's not about where you start or how fast you progress, but about the courage and determination you show in pursuing your dreams and creating a life that is uniquely yours.

www.ingramcontent.com/pod-product-compliance
Lightning Source LLC
Chambersburg PA
CBHW051548250726
48653CB00004BA/1046